Birgitte Stjärne

The Intrapreneur

The Key to Innovation

How to lead

the Dreamers Who Do

Swedish original title: Intraprenören - Nyckeln till innovation

Copyright © Birgitte Stjärne 2018
Photographer cover: Leif Strid, Zebra reklambyrå
Translation: Edwina Simpson
Publisher: Kraftsamlarna Förlag
ISBN 978-91-984462-1-0

CONTENT

INTRODUCTION

The pace of change is accelerating, and advanced technology and expertise are no longer the preserve of a select few. Organisations that do not keep up with developments quickly fall by the wayside. In the long-term, abstaining from innovation is likely to result in severe financial consequences. So, for any organisation aiming at long-term survival, continuous innovation, i.e. the ability to manage constant development and change, is an essential core skill (Steiber 2014).

Globalisation and new technology make it more and more difficult for established companies to combat increasing competition simply by reducing costs and expanding the range of existing products. New entrants into a market introduce competition by renewing existing solutions and developing completely new products and services. It is not uncommon for them to introduce disruptive, radical, changes that fundamentally alter market conditions.

Researchers and industry agree that an organisation's employees, its co-workers, are the most important factor in successful innovation. It is the most creative co-workers, the intrapreneurs, that generate the development and process of revitalisation that businesses and organisations need. Intrapreneurs act as catalysts for change, driving development work in their workplaces. Just as entrepreneurs are needed for innovation in start-ups, creative co-workers – intrapreneurs – are required to drive innovation in established organisations.

In the past, established businesses often fulfilled their need for innovation by buying up or partnering with innovative companies in order to increase their market share and competitiveness. But acquisitions are only effective if what you have acquired can generate even more innovation. For that reason, businesses are now increasingly making use of business accelerators and incubators, often working alongside universities and colleges, in order to benefit from new ideas and the innovative energy of start-ups. This has become a way for businesses to quickly get access to innovation without having to 'disrupt' their own operations with excessive change. But businesses are now starting to look again at their own intrapreneurs.

This is happening partly because the competition between employers to attract the best talent is greater than ever before. At the same time, young people are being increasingly demanding about where and how they work.

The group of young employees known as 'millennials', or Generation Y, are described as a generation of individuals who consider themselves fully entitled to freely pursue their own ideas and want to make a meaningful difference right from the start of their careers (Kruege 2015). According to the *Deloitte Millennial Survey 2016*, between 60% and 70% of all employees in this group expect to leave the organisation they work for within five years, because they do not find their duties sufficiently autonomous, creative or meaningful. If their needs are not met, young people prefer to put their entrepreneurial energy into start-ups. Meanwhile, the survey also shows that many people are in fact prepared to stay on and grow with their current employer if they are given the opportunity to work on their own development projects (Deloitte 2016).

This increasing pressure from younger employees, coupled with the need to manage continuous innovation, requires a broader perspective. Many employers seek personal qualities such as creativity, flexibility, independent thinking and curiosity in their new recruits. They see these as essential for a co-worker who must not only work in a state of constant flux but also needs to be able to contribute to vital development. At the same time, there is greater demand for more intrapreneurs to drive innovation within businesses.

This presents businesses with major challenges. There is often potential for intrapreneurship in people whose skills are not immediately identifiable or quantifiable; also, many organisations fail to change their structures and management so that they can develop and retain their intrapreneurs. That makes it impossible to recruit new staff and means businesses are not able to realise the full potential of their own co-workers.

This is largely due to limited knowledge and experience of intrapreneurship, at least in those organisations for whom innovation is not high on the agenda. In addition, it can be difficult to get access to intrapreneurs' own experiences as it is quite common for intrapreneurs to be unaware that they *are* intrapreneurs. Of those who do recognise themselves as such, few have written down or shared their experiences with others. There are exceptions, in the shape of the small number of intrapreneurs who have become so successful and well-known that their biographies feature on bestseller lists. For the ordinary person, however, it can be difficult both to relate to the experiences of those well-known individuals and to translate them into the practicalities of their own lives. Neither does research provide concrete answers to the question of how intrapreneurs drive innovation in practice and what their everyday lives look like. There are, however, a number of interesting research theories about intrapreneurship and innovation.

Why intrapreneurs are the key to innovation

Most people agree that the unique quality of an intrapreneur is their ability to create and realise their own dreams and ideas while at the same time capturing the dreams and ideas of others. I would say that it is the latter that is the key to successful innovation: the intrapreneur's ability to find words to express dreams and to persuade others – managers, colleagues and co-workers – to go with them on their journey. The seed of all types of innovation lies within those skilled employees who experience meaning, joy and pride in their work and who choose to invest blood, sweat and tears into producing something even better. The intrapreneur acts as a catalyst for the feelings and ambitions of these co-workers.

It took me over twenty years to realise that I was an intrapreneur, in terms of being someone who sees only opportunities with all that that entails. It took a further ten years of self-analysis, interviews with other intrapreneurs and study of various research theories before I became fully aware of the implications of being an intrapreneur. I want to share what I have learned with you because I am convinced that managers can become better at driving innovation with the help of the intrapreneurs in their organisations.

To do this, we need a greater understanding of what it is that motivates intrapreneurs to drive innovation. This book therefore looks at what intrapreneurs have in common and what either connects them with other managers and co-workers or sets them apart. It describes how intrapreneurs experience their day-to-day lives, and how they influence and are influenced by their environment. It also features a review of current research in several areas alongside presentations of the experiences of intrapreneurs themselves. My intention is to bring the thoughts, ideas and knowledge of others together with my own in order to suggest what businesses and organisations can do to become better at identifying, developing and retaining their intrapreneurs. Owners, board members, business leaders, managers, co-workers and intrapreneurs alike will all benefit from the book, which offers both factual reading and a source of inspiration.

Interviews with intrapreneurs

I have interviewed various intrapreneurs – both men and women, with varying backgrounds, positions and experiences – all of whom have provided differing perspectives on intrapreneurship. Three of the interviews are reproduced in their entirety in order to illustrate the different situations in which intrapreneurs operate.

The first interview involves an individual considered by researchers as almost the classic intrapreneur, someone whose thirty-year career incorporates virtually all aspects of intrapreneurship. I use that interview as the starting point for a more in-depth analysis of the more complex and contradictory aspects of intrapreneurship. A second interview shows how things can work in a workplace where most of an intrapreneur's needs are met right from the outset. Finally, one intrapreneur describes the challenges and opportunities that arise when an intrapreneur and an entrepreneur are expected to work together. Names of intrapreneurs and businesses are withheld at their request.

Research

I have aimed in this book to provide the most comprehensive picture of the intrapreneur possible by linking the real-life experiences of intrapreneurs with the theories of researchers. I have chosen to write both about research that is directly linked to intrapreneurship and innovation and about research in many other areas too. The latter considers factors that are important for our understanding of the personalities and contexts of both intrapreneurs and other co-workers. It deals with topics such as the work environment and management, creativity and internal motivation, and how the brain affects will-power, patience and habitual behaviour. For each area, I link the results of the research to my analysis of their significance for intrapreneurs and intrapreneurship.

There is a summary of a selection of the concepts and research theories discussed in the various sections at the end of the book. I also provide references to the various researchers I quote from and whose research, articles and books constitute the theoretical basis of this book

CHAPTER 1

ABOUT INTRAPRENEURS AND INTRAPRENEURSHIP

Employees who drive innovation have been called different things; they may be known as "innovators", "intrapreneurs" or "internal entrepreneurs". It is important to me that a concept is not misunderstood simply because it appears differently in different contexts. Because of this, I choose to use the word "intrapreneur", which is a concept established thirty years ago and which is now increasingly resurfacing in research, literature and the media (Baruah & Ward 2014).

Gifford Pinchot III is an authority in the field of research on intrapreneurs and intrapreneurship, and his conclusions are freely cited by others. From the outset, his focus has been on both intrapreneurship in organisations and the intrapreneur as an individual, which makes his research especially interesting. I therefore begin the book with a summary of Pinchot's various definitions and concepts and a description of his thinking around intrapreneurs and intrapreneurship. This then serves as our starting point for an investigation into the actualities of the intrapreneur.

What is intrapreneurship?

It was Gifford Pinchot and Elisabeth Pinchot who jointly coined the term "intrapreneur" in 1978, as a portmanteau word derived from the expression "Intra-Corporate Entrepreneur." Less than ten years later, it had become an accepted concept in research. In 1985, he wrote the book "Intrapreneurship: Why You Don't Have to Leave the Corporation to Become an Entrepreneur," including a line of argument that was to become key to the debate on innovation in established organisations. In it, he discusses both the personal qualities of intrapreneurs and the characteristics of the intrapreneurial process.

Pinchot (1985) observed thirty years ago that the future would be intrapreneurial and that leaders of organisations would need to be able to manage increasingly complex organisational factors such as internal structures, resources and cultures. He also noted that they would need to manage external factors such as customer demands and competition from the world at large. Pinchot felt that the greatest challenge facing organisations in the future was: *"Finding a way to motivate and keep intrapreneurs [...]"* From being a mere theory, his conclusion has become a reality for companies and other organisations today.

Intrapreneurship can be described as an organisational strategy that integrates risk-taking and innovation and that presupposes a company with an innovative culture. This can in turn help to bring about increases in capacity for innovation, profitability and competitiveness. At the same time, it is important that organisations manage the increased complexity and maintain a balance between innovation and effective leadership of existing operations. The degree of complexity largely depends on the attitudes that dominate within the organisation.

In earlier research, those employees who drove innovation were viewed as a type of entrepreneur operating within the framework of the organisation. They were called "corporate entrepreneurs" and it was felt that they were a way for management to employ an entrepreneurial mindset within large companies (Zahra 1995). So it was management that had the responsibility and initiated innovation in a top-down approach. Pinchot (1985) describes how intrapreneurship is instead based on a bottom-up approach with innovation being initiated by employees at a lower level.

What he means by this is that successful innovation assumes that individual co-workers proactively develop their own work-related initiatives rather than having orders imposed from on high. Researchers Bostjan Antoncic and Robert D. Hisrich (2003) state that intrapreneurship is crucial to organisational and financial development whatever the size of an organisation. "Intrapreneurship should be viewed as a multidimensional concept with focus on (i.a.) new ventures, new businesses, product/service innovativeness, process innovativeness, risk taking, self-renewal, proactiveness, and competitive aggressiveness."

Other researchers, such as Bill Gartner (1989), instead see both the entrepreneur and the intrapreneur as elements of an innovatory process aiming to create a new organisation. Gartner claims that this role requires foresight and proactiveness and the will and ability to identify and create new economic opportunities. The process can be competitive or interactive, and may be characterised by some degree of uncertainty and risk-taking. The goal is linked to some sort of 'internal start-up', and the outcome might be innovation, development and efficiency improvements or a transformation of resources that creates something completely new. That "something new" might be a new company, business unit or sales outlet.

Gartner (2005) believes that what matters is not the intrapreneur as an individual but a particular entrepreneurial behaviour. In his opinion, we should look less at the person and more at the situation and how the person in question behaves. It is what these people choose to do that sets them apart. Entrepreneurs do things that are new and different. They often experience opposition, but they put their ideas into action nonetheless. Things do not always work out right, but things might happen anyway and potentially alter people's perspectives.

Research has taken several different views of intrapreneurship, and for many years the focus was on entrepreneurs and entrepreneurship. As a result, there was little general interest in the intrapreneur as a person until a few years ago. Because of the rising interest in research at the level of the individual, researchers and literature today have linked to the debate that was taking place in the first few years of the 2000s. Various researchers have made different distinctions between the concepts of intrapreneurship, internal entrepreneurship and corporate entrepreneurship (Sharma and Chrisman 1999), but they are now used as largely synonymous concepts to describe in general the innovation driven by employees in established organisations.

Intrapreneurial structure and culture

Pinchot (1985) claims that, since intrapreneurs' goals usually tally with the goals of the business, organisations have just as much to gain by taking advantage of intrapreneurs' ideas as intrapreneurs themselves, or perhaps even more. Organisations should therefore set aside some designated internal capital for intrapreneurship. He believes that the intrapreneurial organisation should be flat and managed in the most unbureaucratic way possible, ideally as if there were several parallel, smaller companies working together. The organisation must also have managers capable of making the most of the intrapreneur's ideas. In his opinion, the most important leadership characteristics in an intrapreneurial organisation are courage, good intuition and an ability to build trust. A manager's analytical abilities are of secondary importance.

In an organisation where the culture is bureaucratic, conservative and rigid, management will not encourage innovation outside the organisation's areas of interests, nor will it be accepting of mistakes. With the organisation at large doubtful, this is not the ideal environment for intrapreneurship, and the intrapreneur's ideas or resources may be subjected to strict controls and restrictions. Intrapreneurship requires the opposite of this – a flexible culture with commitment that allows for the investigation of new ideas, ventures and projects. If there is a lack of communication and a reluctance to test out proposed new ideas, business models or markets, the intrapreneurial spirit may disappear and/or intrapreneurs may leave.

It is in the nature of intrapreneurship to have a decentralising effect on an organisation, so that the focus shifts from hierarchies to individuals. Pinchot therefore sees the organisations of the future as a number of smaller organisations that work in parallel under the same umbrella, which requires a flat, unbureaucratic structure. He believes that the major challenge for management will be to integrate visionary leaders into the organisation while ensuring stability in existing operations. The visionary leaders needing to be integrated will themselves be leading teams of other, restless intrapreneurs ...

Pinchot's conclusions about intrapreneurship from thirty years ago remain largely valid today. Successful innovation is a strategic issue, and the route to achieving it incorporates the intrapreneur's personality, the intrapreneurial process and the structure and culture of the organisation.

These are areas that this book addresses, from both the researcher's and the intrapreneur's perspective.

What kind of people are intrapreneurs?

Pinchot (1985, 1987) sees the intrapreneur as a combination of visionary and implementer in large organisations:

"Intrapreneurs are any of the 'dreamers who do'. Those who take hands-on responsibility for creating innovation of any kind within an organization. They may be the creators, or inventors, but are always the dreamers who figure out how to turn an idea into a profitable reality".

Intrapreneurs thus do not need to be the people who come up with the ideas, but they do assume direct responsibility for creating something new within the organisation. Pinchot (1985) divides the intrapreneur's input into two different areas, one being more theoretical and the other of a more practical nature. He identifies two different phases of intrapreneurial behaviour that he calls "vision and imagination" and "preparation and emerging exploitation".

Bosma, Wennekers & Amoros (2012) describe these phases thus: "The first phase, i.e. 'idea development for a new activity' includes for example active information search, brainstorming and submitting ideas for new activities to the management or the business. The second phase, i.e. preparation and implementation of a new activity, refers to promoting an idea for a new activity, preparing a business plan, marketing the new activity, finding financial resources and acquiring a team of workers for the new activity".

In order to implement different ideas, the intrapreneur forms cross-functional teams and seeks both formal and informal support from other people in the organisation. According to Pinchot, the only way the intrapreneur and their team can achieve success is by getting support from people sufficiently high up in the organisational hierarchy. He identifies two different types of support: that which comes from a "sponsor" or a "protector", or that which comes from both. A sponsor is someone with the necessary resources to clear away organisational, political or financial barriers – perhaps an owner, a CEO or a previous intrapreneur. A protector is normally someone in the senior management team who is open to new ideas.

Although intrapreneurs must be talented managers to be able to bring other, skilled co-workers along with them, Pinchot claims that they are substantially different to normal, traditional managers. He believes that intrapreneurs need to have strong leadership qualities so that they can strengthen the project team and convince co-workers that they need to adhere to and implement their ideas. Positive leadership qualities are also essential if an intrapreneur is to be able to make quick decisions in uncertain circumstances. This, Pinchot claims, is the exact opposite of how normal managers operate, as most managers keep a close eye on risks, avoid uncertainty and often work only within established limits. It is his opinion that normal managers get their authority from above, while intrapreneurs themselves set processes in motion without having been granted power to the same extent.

What are the characteristics of an intrapreneur?

Intrapreneurs are constantly challenging the status quo; they are aware and curious and always itching to get involved. For them, there are always better ways to do things, and things that could be done differently. Intrapreneurs see opportunity in everything and are driven by internal motivation to realise their ideas by creating something new and at the same time to develop as individuals and learn. Innovation can involve everything from new products or services and improved processes to a completely new business model and new markets.

Some researchers are sceptical about the concept of the intrapreneur as they think that the differences between different individuals working in different organisations are too great to be covered by a single idea. Pinchot (1985) also perceives a difficulty in establishing a precise definition of the qualities that characterise intrapreneurs. He associates the intrapreneur with a strong will and ability to act, and believes that a person may sometimes "just become an intrapreneur" because circumstances drive them to it. For Pinchot, will is crucial, because if the will to do something new is sufficiently strong, education, age and position within the organisation are of no importance.

In terms of the intrapreneur's personal qualities, Pinchot claims that personality and skills are more important than the quality of the ideas. In his opinion, personality does not change as quickly as a business plan does. An intrapreneur's personality is, therefore, highly important. If intrapreneurs are to capitalise on their personality and intuition to the full, and develop and perform to their maximum capacity, they must be given freedom to act.

At a broader level, researchers Jeroen de Jong and Sander Wennekers (2008) analyse the concept of intrapreneurship by focussing on employees' proactivity, innovative work and behaviours. They identify concrete activities related to intrapreneurship and the various behaviours that they consider to be associated with the undertaking of such activities. For these researchers, intrapreneurial activities include:

- opportunity perception
- idea generation
- designing new products or concepts
- forming strategic alliances
- convincing management
- mobilising the necessary resources
- planning and organising

They link these activities to the way the intrapreneur acts, which might be:
- out of the box thinking
- taking initiative
- networking behaviour
- taking charge
- perseverance and wilful behaviour
- getting the job done
- some degree of risk-taking

Using Pinchot's original definition as their basis, de Jong and Wennekers divide intrapreneurship into three phases rather than two – Vision and imagination; Preparation; and Emerging Exploitation – but see them mainly as a theoretical model for research. They are of the opinion that, "in reality, these phases overlap, and sometimes activities are partly carried out in recurring cycles and/or in a reversed order." It is only recently that researchers have begun to take more of an interest in the intrapreneur's personal or individual qualities, motivations and behaviours. Even today, they are studied mainly on the basis of the entrepreneur model, probably because there is a good deal of collected data about entrepreneurs. It is of course always difficult to make a case for any absolute truths about the characteristics of a particular type of personality. One aggravating circumstance I would note is that, unlike entrepreneurs, intrapreneurs do not themselves always seem to be aware of the role they are playing. When I interview intrapreneurs, it proves relatively simple for them to identify intrapreneurial characteristics in other people around them. Initially, however, most of them are completely or at least partly unaware that they have similar traits themselves. It is not until I give examples of qualities that researchers say are characteristic of an intrapreneur and of the circumstances in which such a person works that they nod in recognition and declare "that's exactly how *I* work".

A question I am often asked myself is, "What distinguishes an intrapreneur from other co-workers, and how you can judge who is, or is not, an intrapreneur?" My answer is that it is to do with that complex combination of qualities, motivations and behaviours found in an intrapreneur. The qualities, for example, are by no means unique in themselves as they are shared by many people, but I would claim that what makes intrapreneurs different is in part the number of qualities and how some of them conflict with each other and in part the strength and intensity of their motivation.

When I compare research theories about the characteristics of intrapreneurs with what emerges in the interviews, the connections between them become quite apparent. There are concepts that feature repeatedly in descriptions of "an intrapreneurial personality." A summary of these shows that intrapreneurs are ascribed many qualities and behaviours that are in general considered positive and "good and useful" for those that possess them. At the same time, it is clear that the same qualities can be interpreted in a very negative way by people who are not appreciative of intrapreneurs and their behaviours.

An intrapreneur may, for example, be perceived as:

Hard-working, analytical, responsible, affirmative, driving, energetic, dedicated, enthusiastic, persistent, flexible, focused, effective, innovative, inspiring, communicative, skilled, creative, receptive, courageous, target-oriented, versatile, curious, optimistic, passionate, positive, selfless, straight, sees opportunities, independent, patient, articulate, strong-willed, visionary, humble and open.

This is a list that has many positive words, but there is another, less positive side to it. In the interviews, several intrapreneurs describe their own experiences of arousing strong feelings in those around them. They are not surprised if they are sometimes perceived as odd, provocative and/or troublesome, even if this is not their intention. So those people who do not see the benefits of what intrapreneurs do may instead see their behaviour as negative and perceive them as:

Impatient, ambitious, insensitive, having their own agenda, assertive, over-talkative, boastful, obstinate, unrestrained, inflexible, fluffy, inconsistent, excessive, dominating, careless, disposed to take risks, unrealistic dreamers

In other words, the qualities and behaviours associated with intrapreneurs are powerfully expressed, whether they are positive or negative. That in itself shows that intrapreneurs as individuals are often noticed or even stick out in the workplace. My conclusion is that, in their eagerness to drive innovation, intrapreneurs are not always fully aware of "the effect they have on their environment" or that their personality may sometimes be a hindrance. Things are not made easier if there is a lack of knowledge and understanding in the rest of the organisation.

Even if in practice the realities of different intrapreneurs vary, it is this complex combination of qualities and motivations that make intrapreneurs unique. Rather than being positive about themselves and feeling valued by others, they may see their differentness as a burden.

It is normal for an intrapreneur to come up against strong opposition in their immediate environment, as innovation means changes in existing processes and tasks, which can create both additional work for colleagues and co-workers and a feeling of insecurity. In addition, there are no guarantees that the outcome will be better and more profitable than what is already being done. Managerial performance is often measured on the basis of how good managers are at getting their day-to-day tasks done and on current levels of profitability, not on potential, future innovations. If, moreover, the intrapreneur does not adhere to the rules and procedures, other problems may arise that disturb various other aspects of the organisation.

If an intrapreneur experiences firm resistance to both their ideas and their personality, the intrapreneur may, in the worst-case scenario, try to adapt to such an extent that a great deal of their innovative energy remains unutilised. But the interviews also suggest that the more experience and success an intrapreneur has, the less they seem to be affected by the attitudes of those around them. If opposition is too strong at a number of different levels, the intrapreneur will leave the organisation and move to a competitor, or start their own business.

I am also asked about what the specific, unique needs are of this group of co-workers. There is no simple answer, other than that intrapreneurs need space and an outlet for their motivation in their work, as work constitutes such an essential and key part of their lives.

From the research and the interviews, we can identify five motivating factors that seem to drive intrapreneurs particularly strongly and that can be reflected in a range of different behaviours. I describe these below and give examples of the behaviours that follow from them.

The five motivating factors mean that intrapreneurs need to:

1. Live their vision

Intrapreneurs create their own vision and put it into words. The vision is often strongly associated with, or integrated into, the organisation's vision and goals.

They do this by:
' Taking a personal stand on the organisation's values, vision and goals
' Identifying needs and opportunities in their work
' Creating their own vision around what is possible
' Formulating and presenting their own ideas and those of others

- Getting others to share their vision and ideas, to see the opportunities
- Inspiring others to work in the same direction

2. Seek challenges and create something new

Intrapreneurs are motivated by challenges, and by improving and developing so as to create something new and different.

They do this by:

- Thinking outside the box
- Questioning existing solutions
- Asking all kinds of questions, including uncomfortable ones
- Challenging the current system
- Driving development in the face of opposition

3. Find solutions to problems

Intrapreneurs are motivated by finding solutions to problems and by the belief that "anything is possible".

They do this by:

- Making use of their own skills
- Seeing what is missing, identifying various needs within and outside the organisation
- Putting into words "how things should be instead", presenting their own ideas and those of others
- Using cross-functional skills as resources
- Creating skilled intrapreneurial teams
- Developing possible solutions alongside other people

4. Freedom

Intrapreneurs are motivated by being able to work independently with a large amount of freedom, without restrictions, rules or procedures and with minimal management and control.

They do this by:

- Questioning and bypassing restrictive standards and rules
- Starting and managing processes themselves
- Working "under the radar" if necessary
- Building relationships with skilled managers, colleagues and co-workers, irrespective of their position

5. Personal development

Intrapreneurs are motivated by change, new knowledge and new experiences. They achieve these by:

- Changing duties, departments and/or post
- Prioritising continuous professional development in a variety of areas
- Sharing experiences with both external and internal contacts
- Changing employer or starting their own business (particularly if they experience internal opposition)

It is only when intrapreneurs are given space to realise their motivation that they are able to create disruptive, continuous innovation, but the strength of their motivation, and thus the ability to innovate, varies from intrapreneur to intrapreneur.

Independent intrapreneur or intrapreneur supported by management?

Not all intrapreneurs have a strong drive and they do not all work in the same way. Some are the drivers of radical change, and some work to bring about improvement and development in small steps. As with Pinchot's theories, other researchers believe that it is possible to be an intrapreneur in varying degrees and to be active as such in different ways. The issues under discussion are the ways in which they differ and whether special circumstances are necessary to persuade intrapreneurs to step forward. One recurring question is whether a person can learn to be an intrapreneur, which Pinchot, of course, believes is possible if the individual is merely strong-willed enough.

Researchers Niels Bosma, Erik Stam and Sander Wennekers (2010) provide two definitions of the intrapreneur concept, one broad and one narrow. Their belief is that many employees may be involved in developing business concepts but that not all of them are intrapreneurs. Their broad definition encompasses all employees who have been actively involved and have had a leading role in at least one of the two phases that according to Pinchot (1985) define intrapreneurship. They are: 1) idea development for new business activities; and 2) preparation and (emerging) exploitation of these new activities. Intrapreneurs defined according to the narrow definition have a leading role in <u>both</u> phases of the intrapreneurial process.

An intrapreneur who is involved in only one of the phases is described by the researchers as "an intrapreneur developed with management support". This is because they are considered to be more dependent on their environment than those who drive the entire innovative process on their own.

Klas Karlsson is the founder and CEO of the Swedish executive recruitment company Talentia, which has been awarding the Intrapreneur of the Year prize since 2009. In an interview in 2014, Karlsson makes a similar distinction, dividing intrapreneurs into two types, which he calls first-grade and second-grade intrapreneurs. The difference between the two, he says, is that different types of contextual factors need to be in place before they will show themselves. In any organisation that does not reward intrapreneurial behaviour, only first-grade intrapreneurs will show their intrapreneurial qualities, because they are strongly convinced that their ideas are correct. They will therefore find ways to put their ideas into action, whether or not they are sanctioned from above. This type of intrapreneur often works in secret without the knowledge of senior management, and will then go on to present a positive innovation.

In addition to that, there is another type of intrapreneur that can be coaxed out with the right stimuli. To persuade these to step forward, the right manager is key. Karlsson believes that a lot of people could become intrapreneurs given appropriate management. An effective process requires a manager who can manage this type of individual instead of writing them off as "troublemakers" and depriving them of the chance to succeed. Stimulating employees to dare to make a mistake and fail creates a structure that motivates an organisation to become intrapreneurial. This is important as individuals within the organisation are then able to take action in respect of issues that management has not yet noticed. In Karlsson's view, it is not possible for an organisation to consist solely of individuals who want to do new things all the time, as that would lead to anarchy.

Identifying intrapreneurs

I conclude that even if many intrapreneurs are themselves aware that they differ in various ways from their colleagues, they are often not aware of the nature of their uniqueness. It is therefore not surprising that people around them find it difficult to identify them and take advantage of their resources. At the same time as management is trying various ways to encourage employees to come up with new ideas and business proposals, they are also searching high and low for new miracle workers from outside the organisation. They are looking for people who are expected to bring to the organisation an ability to generate radical innovations and find new solutions to old problems.

Companies come up against a number of difficulties when they focus on trying to recruit the "right person" from the start. People with obvious intrapreneurial traits may be actively or passively deselected during recruitment because they do not fit the standard template. Meanwhile, it is no less important for companies to identify and make use of relevant individuals from amongst their existing employees – not least because those who are already familiar with an organisation are often up and running much more quickly than anyone recruited from the outside specifically to drive change.

Whether these creative, flexible, independent-minded and enquiring individuals are recruited externally or are "discovered" internally, the organisation will face major, long-term challenges. While the demand for intrapreneurs grows, many organisations fail to develop and retain them. They are unable to change their structures and management so as to create an intrapreneurial organisation. This means it becomes difficult to recruit successfully, and they lose the ability to realise the potential of their own employees.

The CEO of the executive recruitment company Talentia, Klas Karlsson (2014), has witnessed how organisations treated prospective intrapreneurs in some former workplaces. "In every cohort of trainees there would be one or two individuals with a fresh approach and ideas that could have helped bring about a whole new direction for the organisation." However, he says, they were not rewarded in the workplace, often leaving the organisation due to a lack of stimulation as their employer lacked experience of managing their specific skills.

Being an intrapreneur means having special skills and a particularly high degree of motivation. Everyone has skills and motivations, but they differ from individual to individual. Just because an intrapreneur is unique does not mean that they do not share a series of fundamental needs with other co-workers at different levels in the organisation. For example, most employees need some form of support, attention and development and competent, appropriate management.

However, it is essential to be aware that an intrapreneur cannot achieve results on their own. If they are to drive innovation, they need to be able to work closely with managers, colleagues and co-workers who are skilled, engaged and motivated. Crucial factors in achieving real success, therefore, include managers putting the right conditions in place and working with fellow employees to establish a trusting and responsible climate in the workplace.

One way of showing what really marks out an intrapreneur is to compare intrapreneurs with entrepreneurs; this is something I look at in the next section.

Being an intrapreneur or an entrepreneur

It is easy to identify a range of similarities between the personalities of an intrapreneur and an entrepreneur. They are particularly alike in their tendency to spot opportunities and investigate the world around them with curiosity, and in their willingness to take risks. But they also differ on some significant points, and I would claim that the intrapreneur has a more complex combination of qualities. For example, both intrapreneurs and entrepreneurs display passion, will-power, persistence and courage. However, qualities such as selflessness, receptiveness and patience are essential for an intrapreneur but are found only to varying degrees in an entrepreneur. The reason for this is mainly the environment in which such people operate.

An entrepreneur is an innovative person who runs their own business. Entrepreneurs build up their businesses from scratch, pursue their vision and put their ideas into practice. They own, drive and control both their business and innovation, make the important decisions themselves and bear the financial risk. Some entrepreneurs may work with start-ups, others may have progressed further and created a growth company. There is currently a debate in Sweden about how difficult it is for small and medium-sized entrepreneur-led organisations to finance growth and about how entrepreneurs are having to sell their companies prematurely or are choosing to move them abroad (DN 2016).

Intrapreneurs are mainly to be found working as employees in large or medium-sized organisations. They link their vision and both their own ideas and those of others directly to their work tasks, and invest a great deal of themselves and their own ambitions in the future of the organisation. An intrapreneur does not bear a financial risk in the same way as an entrepreneur does. Instead, their greatest challenge is having the patience to handle internal opposition and politics. This is important as they are part of an organisational and hierarchical system in which the crucial decisions are made by other people.

Putting an intrapreneur's ideas into effect often requires significantly greater resources than are normally available in an entrepreneur-led start-up. There may be a need for capital, but other requirements often dominate, such as access to production and marketing resources, knowledge and cross-functional skills. As a result, factors such as management, human resources and the work environment are very important in determining whether or not an intrapreneur is successful.

As the leading figure in the organisation, it is the entrepreneur who is associated with, and financially affected by, the company's results. This is seen as a natural part of the financial risk that the entrepreneur bears. On the other hand, it is still unusual to link an intrapreneur to an organisation's financial results on the basis of their ideas, new concepts and innovative product development.

Intrapreneurs often neither seek nor receive a financial reward for their efforts. However, there are important exceptions, with special reward systems being developed for innovation in strongly innovation-driven businesses and sectors. It is still not uncommon for organisations to realise only at a late stage, if at all, the significant role played by one or more intrapreneurs in creating and driving innovation. The consequence of not providing a intrapreneur with the right conditions in which to work is that they will decide either to "close down" and stop developing, move to a competitor or start up their own business as an entrepreneur. Intrapreneurs will avoid the first alternative as long as they can, but which of the two latter alternatives are they most likely to choose?

Researcher Simon Parker (2009) has looked at what makes people choose either intrapreneurship or entrepreneurship. His work is based on an American study, *The Panel Study of Entrepreneurial Dynamics II* (PSEDII), which aims to increase scientific understanding of the reasons why people start businesses.

Parker defines a "nascent entrepreneur" as "somebody who satisfies all four of the following criteria: 1) they consider themselves to be involved in the firm creation process, 2) they have engaged in some start-up activity in the past 12 months, 3) they expect to own all or part of the new firm, and 4) their initiative has not yet progressed to the point where it may be considered an operating business."

For uniformity, he classifies emerging intrapreneurs in a similar way and adheres to Pinchot's (1985) definition of intrapreneurship. By this definition, intrapreneurs undertake initiatives of their own within an existing organisation with the aim of exploiting new opportunities and creating economic value. In Parker's view, the major difference between an entrepreneur and an intrapreneur is that the latter works on development that relates to their normal work tasks and which is undertaken for the employer.

Parker (2009) divides individual knowledge and skills into "general human capital" and "specific human capital" and asserts that general human capital is associated more with entrepreneurship. Here too he bases his ideas on earlier research that shows that the greater an individual's human capital, the greater their chances of realising their ideas through entrepreneurship.

Parker maintains that general human capital, such as education, proficiency, talents and skills are capabilities that can easily be transferred from organisation to organisation. He gives examples of different types of general human capital: "General human capital is associated with analytical ability, knowledge about business opportunities and conditions, and computational and communication skills." These are capabilities that several employees might possess at the same time. This means that an employee with sound general human capital who puts forward ideas and suggestions for change may find that their employer uses their ideas but lets someone else put them into action. In Parker's view, this is one good reason why a co-worker might instead choose to develop their ideas through a business of their own.

By contrast, specific human capital refers to "certain skills, experience, knowledge and capabilities" acquired though a person's work and "firm-specific training programs." This includes substantial knowledge of a business's internal organisation and how an idea can be progressed through the system. For Parker, the greater an employee's specific human capital, the more logical it may be for them to remain in the organisation to develop their idea.

Parker also identifies factors over and above human capital that are relevant to the choice between intrapreneurship and entrepreneurship. He believes that entrepreneurs work more through direct contact with clients and less on analysing competitors, a state of affairs that arises from both the entrepreneur's social relationships and their general human capital. Parker thus feels that the entrepreneur may have an advantage in the sphere of fast-moving consumer goods (B2C). By contrast, the extensive resources available in the workplace, for marketing, sales and production for example, may be useful to the intrapreneur. At the same time, a strong brand and good reputation as a supplier can be extremely valuable when commercialising B2B activity. Having considered the relationship between entrepreneurs and B2C and between intrapreneurs and B2B, Parker has eventually concluded that it is not, in fact, possible to identify any such clear distinction in practice. He does nevertheless think that, in terms of resources, it may be logical to assume that the entrepreneur has B2C advantages while the intrapreneur has corresponding B2B advantages.

In a later study, Parker and his colleague Matthias Tietz (2012) attempt to identify differences in the motivations of intrapreneurs and entrepreneurs. This work too is based on PSEDII, the American study that aims to increase scientific understanding of the reasons why people start businesses. Their starting point is four motivations believed to be particularly strong in entrepreneurs. Two factors thought important to entrepreneurs (positive factors) are "independence and job autonomy" and "access to good role models". The others are thought unimportant (negative factors), i.e. "recognition and position" and "high incomes and financial security". In the study, the researchers assume that there may be an inverse relationship between what motivates intrapreneurs and what motivates entrepreneurs. The results of the study are not especially convincing, but Parker and Tietz (2012) nonetheless believe that they indicate that further research along these lines is viable.

Similarly, Parker (2009) builds on facts from PSEDII in his observation that there is least interest in entrepreneurship amongst employees under 25 and those over 45. This is the basis for his conclusion that these two age-groups have a greater interest in intrapreneurship than in entrepreneurship. We do not know how relevant Parker's argument about age is to the situation in Sweden, but there have been studies that show that, percentage-wise, there are considerably more Swedish intrapreneurs than entrepreneurs. I will say more about that in the next chapter.

For me, Parker's conclusions are a clear example of how research that is not focused on intrapreneurs is unable to answer the most critical questions. In the studies mentioned above, conclusions are drawn about intrapreneurs on the basis of assumptions about similarities and differences based solely on studies of entrepreneurs. What is missing is the specific nature of intrapreneurship, which is a weakness in current research.

Intrapreneurship and entrepreneurship within organisations

As previously mentioned, there is a good deal more research about entrepreneurs and entrepreneurship than there is about intrapreneurs and intrapreneurship. It is also difficult to assess the value of intrapreneurship, both in Sweden and internationally, as it is not normally possible to infer this from financial reports. This is particularly evident in the fact that the few studies on intrapreneurship that are available do not come up with clear-cut answers, something that became apparent during my examination of the acknowledged studies on the subject.

There is a great deal of researching, measuring and writing relating to how entrepreneurs as business owners contribute to the economic wellbeing of trade and industry and indeed of whole countries. Some of the most comprehensive studies have been undertaken with the help of *The Global Entrepreneurship Monitor* (GEM), which has been looking at how entrepreneurship works in different countries for over fifteen years. The Monitor originally started as a project aiming to look at why some countries were more entrepreneurial than others. The scope of the investigation has increased dramatically, and GEM 2015-2016 surveys over a hundred countries by means of 200,000 interviews. Interviewees are asked questions about entrepreneurial attitudes and behaviour in a specific country and how the national context in different countries affects entrepreneurship.

The GEM defines entrepreneurship as firms started in the past 3½ years, with older firms defined as "established businesses". This distinction is made because entrepreneurship in its earlier phase is thought to make a positive contribution to the dynamics of the economy by introducing new ideas and creating new values. Established businesses instead have an important complementary role to play, which includes providing employment and some stability in the economy having survived the toughest initial years.

In 2008 and 2011, new questions were added to the GEM study relating to employee innovation, so that intrapreneurship could be monitored in different countries and types of economies. The 2008 study was a pilot in which eleven countries were involved in the section covering intrapreneurship. The result of the extended study enabled Bosma, Stam and Wenneker (2010) to present the first international comparative study of intrapreneurship and entrepreneurship at three different levels. The researchers look firstly at the relationship at the macro level between economic development and the incidence of intrapreneurship. At the national level, they compare independent entrepreneurship and intrapreneurship. Finally, at the micro level, the study investigates the different ways in which individual employees develop new business activities for their employers in different countries and how inclined they are to set up their own business.

The pilot study shows that intrapreneurship is approximately twice as common in high-income countries as in low-income countries. The researchers observe that although more than half the intrapreneurs in high-income countries consider themselves sufficiently skilled to start their own business, most of them, at least for a time, choose to remain intrapreneurs. One explanation for this is that, compared to low-income countries, high-income countries offer more skilled work in large organisations and their employees have higher levels of education and therefore greater independence. Factors such as job security and high salaries may also persuade an intrapreneur to remain an employee rather than becoming an entrepreneur. In addition, intrapreneurs have greater expectations of growth in the organisations where they work than those running their own business. Only a third of the intrapreneurs stated that a fear of failing with their own business was preventing them from becoming an entrepreneur.

Sweden was not involved in the first study, but Norway and the Netherlands were included as representatives of high-income countries. The researchers show that, on average, fewer than 5% of employees in the countries studied are intrapreneurs. In most countries, irrespective of income level, the proportion of intrapreneurs is lower than those setting up new businesses, i.e. entrepreneurs.

The second extended GEM study in 2011 involved 52 countries. Bosma, Stam and Wenneker (2012) subsequently presented a study corresponding to the previous one. This divided the countries into three different economies depending on the drivers of growth in the individual country and whether the country competed on price (factor-driven economy), by developing processes and quality (efficiency-driven economy) or by developing new and different products and services (innovation-driven economy). Sweden belongs to the latter group of innovation-driven economies.

The study confirms most of the conclusions of the previous study of intrapreneurship. One new aspect is the more detailed breakdown of the incidence of intrapreneurs. Here, the second study shows that:

- 13.5% of all adults in Sweden have worked on innovation in the past year (i.e., intrapreneurs as defined in GEM 2011)

- GEM indicates that, out of all the countries in the world, Sweden has most intrapreneurs in relation to its number of employees, followed by Denmark, Finland and Belgium

- In other countries in Europe, the proportion of intrapreneurs is around 6-8%, while the average across the world is around 5%

The researchers noted that in 2011, 13.5% of all adults in Sweden were intrapreneurs, the highest proportion of intrapreneurs in the world. The result was analysed, and the Swedish report commented that Sweden and Denmark stood out in comparison to other countries but that, in Sweden, intrapreneurship did not seem to be linked to economic growth. At the same time, it was noted that the proportion of entrepreneurs was low, at only around 6%.

After this study had been accepted, questions about intrapreneurial employees became standard in the GEM studies from 2014 onwards. The results have changed, and in GEM 2014, 2015 and 2016, the proportion of Swedish intrapreneurs declined to halfway down the rankings and is now at only about 6.4%, which was commented on in the 2016 Swedish report.

Closer inspection reveals that, of the 13.5% Swedes who were intrapreneurs in 2011, only half (6.3%) were employed in private companies, and the same applies in Finland. It was subsequently decided that the analysis should report only on intrapreneurs in the private sector, with the result that Sweden no longer stands out in the statistics. However, there is no indication that the premise of the studies has changed, so the reader is obliged to assemble all the pieces of the puzzle in order to understand how it all works.

Another indication that there may be some uncertainty about these figures is the fact that the proportion of intrapreneurs in countries such as Ireland, Norway, Germany and the United States has almost doubled in five years. For example, in 2011 the proportion of intrapreneurs recorded in Ireland was 3.0% while in 2016 it was 6.8%. Whatever the actual level of intrapreneurship in Sweden and other countries and however we want to measure it, it is clear that there is plenty of potential for development in research into intrapreneurship.

However, the most interesting aspect of Bosma, Stam and Wenneker (2012) is that they are the first to attempt to refine their investigations so that they deal solely with intrapreneurship. Their work is cited in almost all reports on intrapreneurship after 2012.

We now need to proceed from the more general level of intrapreneurship to the individual level, on the basis of what I call the intrapreneur's reality. The next section comprises an interview with P, who fits the definition of a successful, radical intrapreneur and whose story has much in common with many other intrapreneurs. To begin with, he did not see himself as fulfilling the criteria to be an intrapreneur, and it was not until we had been talking for some time that he agreed that he probably was an intrapreneur after all. In the interview, P gives a full and generous account of his experiences as an unidentified intrapreneur and what motivates him most.

A radical intrapreneur's story

"Organisations have a great need to keep things neat and tidy within a clear structure, whereas an intrapreneur is someone who cannot stay within the box".

The words of P, a high-ranking technical manager in the European division of an international car parts manufacturer with hundreds of thousands of employees. The company has its own research and development (R&D) units across the world and manufacturing plants in the United States, Europe and China. After more than thirty years with his company as an engineer and middle manager, he has now been part of the organisation's leadership team for a few years. He has a traditional title – technical director – but with the explicit task of acting as the company's visionary and crystal ball.

P travels round the world to the company's various R&D units for discussions with researchers and subcontractors. He questions their customers and their own R&D sections about what they in turn think their customers' needs will be in two, five, or ten years' time. His conclusions now form the basis of many of the company's strategies, those concerning *how* the vision should be achieved.

P is a modest person who does not initially see himself as an intrapreneur. But the more we talk and the more he thinks about his earlier jobs and his career, the more he is persuaded that that is indeed what he is. At the same time, he is at pains to point out that he has never done anything alone; other people, his co-workers, came up with the solutions, he was simply the catalyst, the person who asked the right questions. When I ask him to think about how things are now compared to twenty years ago, he says:

"It's difficult to look back over more than twenty years. At each stage, there were some things that were good and other things that didn't work. Sometimes things started well and then went wrong, but worked out well in the end."

Innovation, for him, is more than just inventing the new, it is also about improvement. To ensure success, you need a manager to support the intrapreneur. P states that managerial support may be given for different reasons, either through genuine interest or for political motives, such as when a local manager wants to be the innovator for the project themselves. He himself has been lucky with the leadership in his companies and often also with his immediate superior. Most managers have been positive about development and open to "going further, doing more, going a little bit further than you'd anticipated at the beginning". P thinks his work is fun, and he does not actively seek out intrapreneurship and innovation – "it just happens". He thinks that it is the situation that triggers a project if the environment is favourable.

P describes himself as someone who "is not afraid of the unknown, likes things to be complicated and is drawn to chaos and disorganisation". It is the fact that no-one can make sense of a thing that attracts him. He gets the chance to do something new and interesting, and hopefully something good will come out of it, though this is not always the case. One cannot know the outcome in advance and must be able to live with the uncertainty. Summing up, P says "This is my life!"

In his view, the manager is very important. "You can't be a nobody at the outset if you don't have the support of your manager, because you won't get anywhere." What sets P apart is that he has done a great deal that was new both to him and to the company. And most of his managers have supported him and encouraged him to explore the unknown. His starting point is usually something he has done previously, and he will then branch off into new things that he has not done before.

For P, an intrapreneur is someone who makes things happen, while the company's leaders and managers are responsible for resources and colleagues contribute their skills. He thinks he offers few concrete solutions himself – the inventing is done by other people – but that his role as an intrapreneur is to find the solutions. He achieves this by asking questions, the right questions! And by pointing out to his managers, "You don't realise how good this could be!" P again states that what motivates him is having the chance to develop. He cannot guarantee that he will generate income for the company, and he feels that he does not have the skills to run the organisation, precisely because he has his own ideas about everything!

Outlining his journey, he describes how, in the 1980s following a tip from a friend, he got a job at a major Swedish company. He could not speak Swedish and had never worked in that sector before, but was lucky enough to encounter a manager who needed someone of his "age, education and motivation". A year passed before he actually started, but he then stayed in Sweden for ten years. He tells of a "fantastic boss" who let him work on anything that was new, things other people did not have time for.

For five or six years, he worked solely on research and prototypes, not on actual production. He had to get to grips with new structures and new concepts, and over time he also learned the practical side of the job. Gradually, he became involved in the company's day-to-day work and contributed a number of good ideas that earned him respect from his co-workers. After a time, he started to use computers to configure important settings, something no-one else was then doing. He worked with a subcontractor who had developed some software and taught P what you could do with it.

Nearly all P's colleagues had issues with the fact that he was working on the software rather than the hardware, but a few years later everyone else was doing the same! He was eventually promoted to a managerial role, and after ten years in Sweden he was recruited by another European company.

When he started in his new post, he had to take over a number of problematic projects. By successfully putting these into production in the European market, he earned the gratitude of clients and as a result came to the attention of company management. Once he had introduced his technical solutions, he noted that one of the systems had not been developed since its launch on the American market ten years previously. He felt that there must be a better way of solving the technical issues, since the current solutions were simply not good enough – so the company had to start development and production again from scratch.

The problems arose when the project progressed from the experimental and prototype stages to the factory for industrial manufacturing. P says that, of the co-workers concerned, whose role was to develop machinery, identify subcontractors and put quality assurance procedures in place, at least half were not interested at all. They did not share the company's vision, feeling that it was "not their problem" to come up with new solutions. In P's words, "everyone found fault, they weren't prepared, lacked experience and were given a whole lot of extra work, which led to a huge amount of opposition. They made their attitudes clear in comments such as, 'It won't work' or 'We haven't done anything like this before'". P says that they could not make it work and were unable to find a way forward because all they could see was a whole lot of problems. However, the senior managers decided that this was the right priority and came to P's rescue, and so the project was implemented in spite of the opposition.

It was easier to work at the US Headquarters than in Europe. In the United States P had support from managers who had known him when he was in Sweden and he was invited to test run an entire new system. Asked a direct question – "What do you think?" – he replied, "Rubbish!". His manager asked him to explain to their fifteen top engineers why this was "rubbish". P was not keen to do this at first, as the people who had developed the system did not know him. But his manager said, "I know you, and that's enough", and called all the engineers to a meeting. P said to them all, "This is what you want! This is what is good and less good about this solution, and if we do this we'll make it better..." One engineer from the group then suggested that it could be done in a different way, involving a specific software solution.

P had not run the system before, but he said to the engineers, "If it's easy to do, then do it". After a couple of days, they came back having redeveloped the software, which now worked. It became clear later that the engineer who suggested the solution had himself clashed with the group and the inventor of the product as they were not willing to listen to his views. With P in place, he took his chance and seized the initiative, and was now able to demonstrate that his thinking had been correct from the outset.

While he was in the United States, P met a previous colleague from Sweden who was now working for one of his company's customers. He also tested the system and agreed that the first version was "rubbish", but said that, following P's suggestions and the changes that had been implemented, it had become "outstanding". So with the seal of approval from a customer, the whole company began to have more confidence in P. However, the Americans were somewhat irritated when P and his company were the first to sell the new system in Europe, before they had got round to it themselves. When it came to adapting the American system to the needs of European customers, P felt that this should not be a stressful process but that they should instead think big. He had not seen the specifications from the European customer, but he was motivated by the difficulty of the challenge.

A couple of years later, just after version number two of the same system had been launched, P was invited to dinner by his manager to celebrate their successes.

In the middle of the meal, P says, he started to talk about version number three and what that ought to involve. His manager was very surprised and initially went very quiet; then, he simply said, "Why?". P explained that the changes he had outlined would make the solutions "so much better [...] if we just...". After five minutes, the manager told him to write down his thoughts and list what he wanted to do, presumably thinking the whole thing would come to nothing. After a couple of days, P had produced a list of the things he wanted to do.

It took a year before work started because of a senior manager who opposed the project and put a stop to it. This was someone who needed to understand all the detail before he would give the go-ahead, which he refused to do. After a year, that manager retired and the project could get started. When P picked up the question of the development project with his immediate managers again, they were also very surprised and sceptical. They had just produced something that their European customers were extremely happy with and which was starting to make a profit. Why would they want to *disrupt* their work by developing something no-one was asking for? But P did not accept his managers' view and objected. He could see no limits to the technical solutions himself, and refused to be content with things as they were. He explained his thinking by saying that, in three or four years' time, their customers would be asking for completely new solutions and so they should start developing them now.

As P's managers knew him by now and knew that he was motivated by making things even better than they were, they let him carry on. The way he puts it himself is that he was being allowed to continue "under the radar". He now needed to find out what was required to overcome the limitations of the current system. That led him to get in contact with the researchers who had produced the original version ten years earlier. It turned out that they had numerous ideas for development but that, up to now, no-one had asked their advice or shown any interest. P sketched out an alternative solution and then got in touch with other people in the organisation. Soon, he had assembled a group of about ten people who shared his frustration over the limitations of the current system but who had assumed that they would have to "live with them". His colleagues had themselves been thinking about what might be possible, and so when P explained how they could develop the product, take it further and make it even better, they listened. They subsequently developed a completely new solution – version 3.0.

At the same time as he was getting the work underway with his colleagues he encountered considerable internal opposition from a large number of co-workers and managers who were content to stay in their comfort zone. They did not want to have their work disrupted, quoted *"better is the enemy of good"* at him and said that there were insufficient resources to achieve the best possible result. P also found that the company's need to create orderliness and structures around its day-to-day work limited opportunities to develop, which he found frustrating.

When the proposal eventually reached the management team in the parent company, the initial reaction there too was extremely sceptical.

"If you change things again, how can we *be sure* that it'll be a success? As we don't know anything, we won't do anything!" Again, people asked him, "We're successful now; why should we disrupt everything? Why reinvent something that already works?" Even the customers were doubtful to start with. When they heard about the ideas, most of them observed, "We haven't asked for this – we don't need anything better than what we've already got". Later, when they saw the prototype of the new system, their responses were very different: "This is fantastic, we had no idea this was possible".

Version 4 of the product is now on the market and is responsible for a third of the company's total sales. Since it also generates most of the company's overall profit, it had the effect of changing P's situation entirely. Now, when he gets an idea or wants to make a change to a project, e.g. to widen its scope, he explains this to management and gets the go-ahead!

When he outlines his ideas for development, he is always careful to give reasons why he thinks something is not as it should be. He thinks "you have to say if something is lacking, that something is missing, which means it's 'rubbish'. You don't get anywhere by doing nothing". It can sometimes be particularly difficult to produce something good. One of P's products, for example, took fifteen years to develop. There may also be an issue with overall resources. Sometimes, when he mentions his various wishes to his managers, they will say, "Yes, but we haven't yet done what you asked us about three years ago ...", and P then simply has to wait and accept that there are not enough resources to go round.

People often say to him, "No-one else could possibly want that!" P replies that this is not true – it is just that other people don't yet know that they want it! He says it is as if he has had "a taste of the future", i.e. got a feel for what the new solution will bring. Before, he would ask his managers, "Can I talk to other customers about this?" but would be told, "No, stay here!", as they felt they were not able to deliver at the same rate as P was presenting possible ideas and solutions to customers. Now, he no longer seeks permission every time. P describes this as creating a need in his customers! He puts together a high-level specification setting out what is required – "If it's at all realistic, I'd like ..." – thinking solely of functions that, purely objectively, do not yet exist. He hands this over to the engineers who produce whatever it is that does not exist. But there is a danger with this, because if you ask the customers they will initially say that they do not need a new solution. However, once they have "had a taster" they are only interested in the new solution and want to know how quickly it can be put into production.

At the same time, P understands management's caution – "if it's currently working, don't change it" – as it is the income from current products that pays for development projects. "Sometimes making cost savings is the only thing that matters!" So as a way of gaining acceptance for the constant changes, it was decided to call the new solutions version 2.0, 3.0 etc.

When asked how he is perceived by the people around him, both at work and in his personal life, he replies, "People around you think you're bragging when you talk about your job and your ideas. But you can't survive as an intrapreneur unless your manager, at least, recognises your worth, and realises that your thinking is *magic*. We [intrapreneurs] don't know how it works ourselves, how all the information and facts gather in your head and then come out in a different form. So you need to be lucky with your managers."

P thinks that you probably have to be a bit naive, optimistic, stupid and mad to take on tasks and projects that no-one else wants or is able to do.

It was the intrapreneurial team, rather than P himself, that started the work on the latest version (4.0), and some of the team have now come forward as intrapreneurs themselves. P describes what happens: "They come to me and ask 'Can we do this? Can the company cope with it? Is it possible?' They don't ask if their idea is a good one, they just want to know if I can help them sell the idea! The team has developed its own energy!"

The company has now reorganised the way it works to make innovation easier. P says that this is not down to him, but I would say the opposite is true. What he brought to the company, over and above his technical expertise, was comprehensive knowledge of the market, a survey of customer needs and a crystal ball, i.e. a means of putting forward ideas about the future.

P is currently working on future development with two co-workers, who are as "stupid and mad" as he is. He tells them that they must not do any testing unless they have a hypothesis or theory to be tested. No "let's just see"; things have to be done "for a reason". P says you must keep asking "Why?" until you find the answer. He claims that, even if nothing useful results, you will have learnt something interesting along the way. It is the journey that is most important. These days former co-workers often come to P and ask his opinion about projects that he is not involved in. They want to know what he thinks about their ideas, and for P this is fantastic.

For the past couple of years, P has been a member of the management team, where he is responsible for developing ideas for the future and discussing "advance sales" with customers. His work has led to a new vision for the company that is no longer just about "What do we do?" but also about "How do we do it?". Discussions about strategy are now also about product development and strategies for what should be sold where/in which market and which new markets the company should aim to penetrate – not, as they were previously, mostly about how much money could be earned from existing products and markets.

P is pleased to be part of these discussions and to be able to help to formulate visions, build the company in line with the needs of the customers and interpret the future. P loves to get recognition, and admits that he has an ego! Nonetheless, it is still the opportunity to develop that is most important to him. Innovation requires managers who listen, allow middle management to have ideas and do not put a stop to ideas coming up through the organisation. Managers need to understand that they do not know – and are not able to do – everything themselves and must be willing to accept their subordinates rising up the ranks. This requires a special culture throughout the organisation so that everyone feels able to say what they think.

Over the years, P has also had one or two managers who he has not been able to work successfully with, and on a couple of occasions has almost been fired for something he did or did not do. Sometimes he spoke out to say that he did not want to do certain things and disobeyed orders because he *knew* that it would not work. He was awkward, because he did not obey orders if he felt they were wrong. Some managers found this challenging, even though he explained why he could not do as he had been asked. The people around him saw what was happening and some colleagues were influenced by P's reasoning and also started to speak out. That meant P was a threat, because he was too strong and giving out the wrong signals. He realises that, particularly at the beginning, he was seen as awkward by people around him who did not understand him. When he started, two or three people knew him and supported him, while others did not understand how valuable he was at all.

"Little dictators, the sort of people who keep co-workers quiet and fearful, shouldn't be allowed," says P, emphatically. However, he does note that it can, unfortunately, be difficult to remove that type of manager, as they have often been in post a long time and achieved good financial results.

Even now, P often meets with reactions such as, "You can't be serious!" when he describes what he has done or how he sees possible new ventures. Some people around him perceive him as excessive, boastful and possessed of a big ego, as they are unable to make sense of what he describes. He does not see anything strange in this as he is only describing his own reality and what he has already achieved. It is common for people to say to him, "You didn't know this, you didn't know that it was going to happen!" His response to this is, "I knew, but not when … I believe that it will happen. It's not crazy, it's what life is like. Life sends us flashes of inspiration, the question is whether or not you notice them."

He describes his internal process as follows:

> It's an instinct, an ability to gather facts and view them in a different way. Whenever I hear a customer or colleague saying 'I'd like a …', it gets fixed in my mind. After a while I'll get a trigger; it comes upon me like a flash of lightning, and I know what I need to do and that it isn't too late to do something."

He continues: "But you need to have patience because it takes time; we have goals but it still takes time."

I ask him if he recognises himself in my description of the intrapreneur as a catalyst in a range of processes. He replies: "Yes, because there is energy there but it is undirected; things are chaotic, and that's a good thing. The less orderliness there is, the greater the chance that something unexpected will happen." He says that it is not about potential: what is important is to be open to finding new ways to combine:

- Differences
- Chaos
- Energy (not power)
- Dynamism

These processes are obstructed by those in the organisation who like to establish clear structures and who advocate organised processes and the giving of orders. P makes a comparison with the biggest difference between people and robots as they currently operate.

> "Only human beings can provide creativity, craziness and the ability to ignore an instruction or an existing process – robots can't do that!"

P says that his current manager endorses him. "He likes me, he sees what I do and he believes in me." At the same time, he would like P to write down how he does things, i.e. record the process he goes through to find new solutions so that other people can do as he does. His manager finds it frustrating when P says he is unable to do that.

In my view, P is describing his process when he says:

- I see a need and can explain what it consists of.
- I am the optimist that believes it is possible.
- I ask the questions.
- I start it off, and other people do the work.
- I can't say that I did it, but I controlled it and made it possible.

At the company they now realise that P's ideas will be put into effect, but they do not know when, how or in what form – they only know that it will happen. This means that the company's management team would like a timetable or delivery schedule, but P cannot provide one. Instead he says, "Wait until I get my flash of inspiration!"

In his view, everything depends on the combination of the "flash", experience and intuition.

Saying, "It just happens" can make the people he works with incredibly irritated, to the extent that they think, "What's the matter with him?"

P has learnt now that he cannot force his suggestions and ideas through if people do not understand what he means. There is no point in applying pressure, you just have to wait, be patient and let the right moment arrive. If his reasoning does not work, he sees it as a lesson in humility. "If no-one understands me, but I think I'm right, I have to think about how I'm communicating. What am I missing, what's wrong, what's preventing them from understanding?" And if something is very important to him, he will seek out other ways to explain that will help them to understand.

Thus concludes P's account of his life as an intrapreneur. In the next section, I highlight qualities, motivating factors and behaviours that feature in both what P has described and what other intrapreneurs have told me when describing their reality.

An intrapreneur's reality

Comparing the interview with P with my own experience and that of other intrapreneurs, I find there are many more similarities than differences. The motivations and behaviours described are very similar, and even the words used are surprisingly alike. What emerges overall is a common picture of how different intrapreneurs experience their own reality, both the positives and the negatives.

I think it is important to highlight different perspectives, both how the intrapreneur sees him or herself and how they might be perceived in their organisation. It is undoubtedly the case that those co-workers closest to the intrapreneur are often extremely positive about them as a person. Colleagues and co-workers at more of a distance may, however, have more doubts or may even be negative, and for the immediate superior the intrapreneur often presents a challenge. I believe that it is only by identifying and highlighting the differences that we can make up our minds about them and thus pave the way to better understanding between the various stakeholders.

The points below are derived from my interview with P and illustrate various phenomena that I outlined in my introduction to various researchers, Pinchot at the forefront. They represent a variety of factors that researchers believe are very important for intrapreneurship.

The intrapreneur within the organisation

P: "Organisations have a great need to keep things neat and tidy within a clear structure, whereas an intrapreneur is someone who cannot stay within the box."

People with strong intrapreneurial tendencies often find it difficult to fit in with hierarchical systems and groups. They like to challenge rules and procedures and seem to find it difficult to submit to authority. If they think there are good reasons to endorse certain rules or individuals they will do so, but otherwise they will not. Whether reasons exist or not is largely based on their own assessment of the situation.

Underpinning the intrapreneur's entire approach is their strong commitment and identification both with their own work and the organisation as a whole. When P says "This is my life", he is expressing something that many intrapreneurs will recognise: complete loyalty to the task and its higher aims, combined with a very strong will and a focus on opportunities. The interviews reveal that the intrapreneurs often feel they are "contributing to a greater good" than personal gain and their own career.

Even if they appreciate being recognised and acknowledged, most intrapreneurs are driven more by internal motivation than material reward. This is something that can be difficult for the people around them to accept, not least if their own motivations are different. The total commitment that an intrapreneur displays can also sometimes be both confusing and frustrating; it can be a challenge to work with someone who seems to have an almost altruistic attitude to their work.

Much research is currently underway on the subject of different types of motivation, something I will return to in the next section. Researchers Edward Deci and Richard Ryan (2000) have shown that many employees are driven to a large extent by external motivations. That external motivation is described as a desire for reward from sources outside oneself. It might be higher wages or other benefits, or a higher-level post and higher status. Researchers say that people driven by internal motivation are largely governed by a sense of meaningfulness and personal development. Many, meanwhile, are driven by a combination of external and internal motivation.

It is perhaps not surprising that people around an intrapreneur may question whether their commitment is completely sincere if they also perceive them as someone who boasts about themselves. P puts it this way: "People around you think you're bragging when you talk about your job and your ideas. But you can't survive as an intrapreneur unless your manager, at least, recognises your worth, and realises that your thinking is magic."

He says that some people around him perceive him as excessive, boastful and possessed of a big ego, as they are unable to embrace what he is describing. Other intrapreneurs report being accused of hubris and megalomania. Several of them mention the "Who do you think you are?" attitude, how no-one should believe that they are better or more important than anyone else. When P "simply describes his own reality and what he has already achieved," some people he encounters choose to interpret this as untruth and/or boasting, as what he is saying is beyond their grasp.

If people around intrapreneurs do not even believe their account of what they have done, the natural outcome may, of course, be suspicion, questioning and a lack of confidence on both sides. It can also mean that an intrapreneur stops talking about their work and dreams, hampering their ability to innovate and to engage others.

Obviously all intrapreneurs are different, and while some are more overt with their activity, others may work away on their own without telling anyone. However, their drive to succeed means that sooner or later they will have to present their ideas to their colleagues. The most visible intrapreneurs are those who are most independent in the least innovative environments, as they most clearly diverge from the workplace norm.

P says of himself: "You have to be a bit naïve, optimistic, stupid and mad to take on tasks and projects that no-one else wants or is able to do". Any other intrapreneur would understand that exactly. Words such as "naïve" and "stupid" have a less than positive ring for those who interpret them negatively, but, for the intrapreneur, what they say is that you have to dare to be different and to go beyond the boundaries of what is acceptable, dare to believe in things that seem impossible and take on the challenge of creating something new. And optimism is absolutely essential to the creative process.

The intrapreneur may, however, pay a high price if the people around them choose the negative interpretation and use this to label them as a person. At greatest risk is the intrapreneur who does not realise he or she has an intrapreneurial personality. It can be devastating for their self-confidence if other people see them as a "nice, but rather naïve and credulous person" rather than acknowledging the skills of the individual in question.

The intrapreneur's internal processes

P: "Whenever I hear a customer or colleague saying 'I'd like a …', it gets fixed in my mind. After a while I'll get a trigger; it comes to me like a flash of lightning, and I know what I need to do and that it isn't too late to do something."

For P, it feels as if all the information and facts assemble in his head and emerge again later in a different form. It's an instinct, an ability to gather facts and view them in a different way. The description closely resembles how other intrapreneurs describe the process – as seeing challenges and problems in a different way and then making things happen.

The word "catalyst" is commonly used by intrapreneurs to mean that they see themselves as someone who believes something needs to happen and who asks the right questions. The individual process described by P tallies well with other descriptions of how intrapreneurs:

- See needs and can express them in words
- Believe that anything is possible
- Ask lots of questions
- Start and control processes
- Secure necessary resources and create teams

All the intrapreneurs stress that they are unable to achieve anything by themselves and that they are dependent on having a team of skilled colleagues and co-workers to come up with various solutions.

It is difficult to put into words what actually occurs when an intrapreneur finally realises that they have found the solution to a problem. Some might describe it as an "Aha!", a gut feeling or a euphoric "Eureka!" moment. P is the only one of them to call this moment a "flash of inspiration", which I think is a wonderful way of describing what happens at the point when everything falls into place. The phrase he uses is, "Wait until I get my flash of inspiration!" Because everything depends on the combination of the "flash", experience and intuition."

Complying with standards and rules

P: "The company's need to create orderliness and structures around its day-to-day work limits opportunities to develop."

Intrapreneurs are careful to emphasise and comply with any rules they themselves feel have particular merit. These might include a strong sense of justice and fair play, an expectation that everyone in the group will "contribute and take a position" or that people listen respectfully to other people's opinions before they make a decision. Rules and procedures are otherwise often felt to be an unnecessary bureaucratic burden that take up time and energy and limit room to manoeuvre.

The intrapreneur would see this purely in logical terms. A rule is only important if it is thought that it will benefit, or fulfil a function for, the project or the organisation as a whole. Some people might see this as the intrapreneur being provocative in that they are not complying with the organisation's ground rules. The approach may irritate those who think rules and control are important and lead them to feel insecure.

Similarly, a person, for example a manager, is valued not for their role, title or status but for the skills and benefits that the intrapreneur feels they bring with them. In terms of authorities and hierarchies, an intrapreneur may sometimes choose to obey a person who is not a manager but who demonstrates great expertise in their area – at the same time as doing everything they can to bypass their own manager, if the manager is not positive about innovation, by working "under the radar".

This rational, utilitarian way of thinking about rules and hierarchies creates behaviours that may lead people around the intrapreneur to see them as inconsistent. In the worst-case scenario, the immediate manager may feel that the intrapreneur is unreliable and even disloyal. In such circumstances, the intrapreneur may sometimes be completely unaware of the effect they are having on others.

Naturally, the extent to which this character trait is apparent in day-to-day work varies from person to person. Over time, a successful intrapreneur becomes skilled at manoeuvring within the complexities of an organisation. A lot of energy is used up on both accommodating and working contrary to rules and regulations and hierarchies. If an intrapreneur chooses to stay and drive innovation, it is an indication that organisational structures are functioning reasonably well and that the intrapreneur can work with them.

Managers who are controlling, obsessed by prestige or who worry greatly if not all the rules are followed rarely have intrapreneurs in their teams.

About chaos

P: "I'm not afraid of the unknown, I like things to be complicated and am drawn to chaos and disorganisation".

P says that chaos can be defined as energy that is already there but which is undirected. "Things are chaotic, and that's a good thing." Seeing chaos as good and even essential is a tendency that intrapreneurs have in common. However, in the eyes of the people around them, it may seem as if intrapreneurs are drawn to chaos or create it themselves. Outsiders might perceive their world as chaotic as there is always a lot going on around them and their team. This is rarely a problem for the team, whose motto might be "the less orderliness there is, the greater the chance that something unexpected will happen". By contrast, people respect and cooperate with each other and everyone contributes their knowledge, commitment and ideas.

P sees it as a chance to "do something new and interesting, and hopefully something good will come out of it, though this is not always the case. You can't know the outcome in advance and have to be able to live with the uncertainty." Researchers tell us that chaos is a prerequisite for creativity and thus for innovation, and this is something you can read more about in later chapters.

Planning and structure

P: "My manager wants me to write down how I do things, i.e. record the process I go through to find new solutions so that other people can do as I do."

P is unable to produce timetables or delivery schedules, neither can he provide a written record of his own processes. When management ask him, he replies that he "*can't* do that, he has to wait for a 'flash of inspiration'". And as he notes himself, it can make people around him extremely irritated when all he can say is that things "just happen". But he is not alone. Many intrapreneurs find it difficult to produce detailed, long-term action plans, not despite the fact that they are very focused but precisely because that is what they are. They know that everything is going to change anyway and that real life does not follow a plan, and so planning is seen as restricting. Instead, intrapreneurs constantly monitor what is happening against their vision and goals and check things off against the outside world. They make continual adjustments and take any necessary action in response to their monitoring.

Some people around intrapreneurs think that planning is essential and that, at the very least, management needs something to steer by. This means that intrapreneurs who refuse to make firm promises for the future may be seen as difficult and deviating from the norm. (So it often happens that intrapreneurs are required to devise the plans that managers ask for but seldom follow them in practice.)

Opposition within the organisation

P: "We are successful now; why should we disrupt that? If you change things again, how can we *know* that it'll be a success? As we don't know anything, we won't do anything!"

The view that you should not change anything that is currently working, at least not if it is profitable, is one that is widely held. It is the rule rather than the exception for intrapreneurs to meet with opposition when they put forward ideas for innovation within an organisation. This is partly because innovation worries co-workers, as the process of developing something new often leads to extra work and risk-taking – perhaps not very surprising given the fact that it is the existing operation that has to finance the new venture. According to the intrapreneurs I have spoken to, the more radical the change, the stronger the opposition.

P, for example, described how he ran into problems when the project progressed from the experimental and prototype stages to the factory. "At least half the people were not the slightest bit interested. They didn't share the company's vision, they felt it was 'not their problem' to come up with new solutions." Many intrapreneurs report that, when they try to start up something new, they encounter negative attitudes such as, "It won't work" or "We haven't done anything like this before".

Intrapreneurs often have close contact with customers and it can be the customers who support and drive the project forward when the intrapreneurs are having to deal with opposition within their own organisation. But where the changes are revolutionary ones, not even the customers can be relied on. P says that the customers themselves sometimes protest against the idea of change, saying, "We haven't asked for this – we don't need anything better than what we've already got".

The role of senior management

P: "I've been lucky! Most of my managers have been positive about development and open to going further, doing more [...] than I'd anticipated at the beginning".

One thing that all the intrapreneurs I interviewed were in agreement on is that intrapreneurs need express support from senior management. As has been mentioned, even if they work under the radar there always comes a point when they need to sell the idea to the rest of the organisation. In order to ensure acceptance and bypass opposition, senior management must express its support. Intrapreneurs do not themselves use concepts such as sponsors and protectors, but the implications of what they describe are the same. A senior manager can either put things in place to enable the intrapreneur to succeed or prevent them from doing so. In P's opinion, what is required is "senior executives who listen, allow middle management to have ideas and do not put a stop to ideas coming up through the organisation. There also needs to be a special culture throughout the organisation so that everyone feels able to say what they think". It is particularly important that the intrapreneur's own manager is recognised and rewarded for the innovative aspects of their work and not just for their measurable operational achievements.

Intrapreneurial cross-functional teams

P: "Soon I'd assembled a group of about ten people who shared my frustration about the limitations of the current systems ..."

P describes how he approached skilled colleagues, researchers and customers by various routes and how, after a while, several team members themselves came forward as intrapreneurs. The interviewed intrapreneurs are unanimous in their view that the team is crucial to the intrapreneur's success. Without the team, there can be no innovation, a fact that is acknowledged in the approach to recognition and reward. It is important that intrapreneurs get validation and recognition for their input, but it is even more important that their teams are validated and acknowledged for the work they put in together. No less essential are the resources needed to progress the project.

The outcome of the processes and the projects are of course very important, but it is particularly important that co-workers are given recognition for their input. It is therefore essential to celebrate successes, preferably together with the whole organisation. This acts as an important their colleagues and co-workers. While many of them are not aware that they are intrapreneurs themselves, they can spot intrapreneurial characteristics in other people.

People around them may feel that the intrapreneur lacks self-belief or that they do not have the drive and/or ability to compete with other people.

These are several examples of qualities and behaviours that, while natural for many intrapreneurs, can be interpreted in different ways by the people around them. What I see as contradictory in this is that the same person has personal qualities and behaviours that seem from the outside to be mutually opposed. For example, intrapreneurs will exercise firm control but are not keen on planning, and they can be both flexible and focused at the same time. They sell their vision by constantly telling others about it, and get information by consciously listening. As a visionary, they see the whole picture but they are also careful to ensure there is structure and quality in the detail. Intrapreneurs are also very strong-willed and driven but very patient, and they can be both self-confident and humble.

These examples clearly show how this kind of person can make great demands on the people around them just because of the way they are. The same intrapreneur may flourish and innovate successfully in one organisation and feel misunderstood and constrained in another.

My aim is to create a greater understanding of, and knowledge about, similarities and differences to make it easier for co-workers to communicate with each other and work together. I hope that this additional knowledge will reduce the frustration and irritation of co-workers and also create a better environment for the intrapreneur's pursuit of innovation. Of course, it is not just personal qualities and drive that affect an intrapreneur's ability to innovate; there are many more factors that come into play. Additional influences include creativity, motivation and the work environment, colleagues and co-workers and, not least, management. I cover these various areas in the next section.

marker, even if the intrapreneur themselves will rarely pause for longer than a moment to celebrate what they see as merely an interim goal on the pathway to achieving their vision.

Contradictory and different

On page 19, I list a number of personal qualities generally ascribed to intrapreneurs and also note that there may be other, less flattering interpretations of an intrapreneur's personality. I have returned to the subject in further sections, where I make the claim that intrapreneurs have a complex combination of qualities, motivations and behaviours and that some conflict between these make intrapreneurs different from other people.

To explain what I mean by that, I now describe a number of qualities in more detail, providing interpretations that are both positive and negative. This should increase the reader's understanding of how such a person might behave, although there are no generalised statements suggesting that all intrapreneurs operate in a certain way.

Alongside the qualities listed below are examples of how they may affect an intrapreneur's behaviours and of how the latter might be perceived by other people.

An intrapreneur is often:

Flexible
An intrapreneur may express a clear opinion or make a decision but then do something that appears to be the exact opposite of what they have just said. This is in line with their constant adjusting of interim goals and resources in response to the world around them, with their focus always on their vision. People around the intrapreneur may see their flexibility as uncertainty. They may perceive them as uncertain, conflicted and unpredictable and may be critical of what they see as a lack of order and consistency.

Focused
Intrapreneurs have an ability to concentrate and be completely focused. This can mean that, at times, they scarcely communicate with the outside world, preferring to investigate and analyse things in isolation on their own territory.

As a result, they may easily forget or block out their daily duties if not reminded, as their focus is on something "more important".

People around the intrapreneur may feel that they do not have time for them, while others will think that they are not attending to all their obligations as they should.

Communicative

Intrapreneurs are committed, often think aloud and may assume that people around them are following their reasoning. When they are at their most inspired, their talk is a way of sharing their thinking and ensuring others are engaged. It is not always clear how much time they spend listening to others. The listening is important for making sure the intrapreneur gets input to help them develop new ideas.

People around them may claim that intrapreneurs talk too much, take up too much space and do not listen.

Creative

Intrapreneurs are a little bit "odd" and think differently because of their creative focus. When new ideas, opportunities or information come along to influence thinking on how the goal might be achieved in the best, most effective way, intrapreneurs change or adjust their resources and interim goals accordingly.

People around them may think that intrapreneurs are "strange" as they are never satisfied. It might be that they believe that it would be more efficient to select a single solution or a solution that already exists rather than expending energy on continually reinventing the wheel.

Courageous

Intrapreneurs are not afraid to challenge existing systems, solutions or authorities. They are analytical and ask awkward questions that challenge those around them, acting as a sort of catalyst that triggers processes. Intrapreneurs do not have all the answers, but they do seek them out and find them, and they are willing to risk trying out different options even if they seem impossible.

People around them may feel intrapreneurs are disrespectful, arrogant and reckless.

Optimistic

Intrapreneurs are optimistic in most situations and are more likely to see opportunities than limitations. That can make it difficult to set limits on their investigation of different options as they do not like to miss anything out. Being constantly open to new initiatives and encouraging others to try out new thinking and ideas sparks off a lot of new processes that are often cross-functional. At the same time, it can also be easy to start up too many projects, or to make them too broad, so that the intrapreneur is unable to finish them all on time.

People around them may feel that the intrapreneur is poor at prioritising and is doing the wrong things, while others may feel that they are encroaching upon their territory and interfering with their work.

Focused on the ultimate goal

The moment the intrapreneur has formulated a new idea or vision in their mind, they are already at the finish line. The process may take the form of a sort of reverse journey during which others may find it difficult to follow a route on a sometimes unclear map. At this stage, the detail is of less importance; it is the vision and the idea that are key.

People around them may become demotivated when they do not get to know or understand the detail of how they are to reach the goal. Those who do not like uncertainty will often insist that the old system or product is working well. Some may choose not to do anything at all, while others may be openly critical and oppose the change.

Curious

Intrapreneurs discover and explore new problems and challenges, in so doing opening up new opportunities. They ask questions and challenge anyone who says something is impossible or will not work. Intrapreneurs will always find the new contacts, new knowledge or interesting depth or breadth that are needed for even better solutions.

People around them may find all the questions and challenging tiresome. They may perceive the intrapreneur as uncertain, or feel inadequate themselves. Others may feel that the intrapreneur interferes in matters that are nothing to do with them.

Passionate

Intrapreneurs are often intense people who will passionately defend their ideas and plans using lots of words and pronounced body language. Their eyes glitter with curiosity when they encounter a challenge or are in a position to ask questions. They may display clear signals and emotions in the form of, for example, joy and optimism in the event of success or frustration and obvious disappointment at set-backs.

People around them may feel uncomfortable at open displays of emotion and see this as a lack of self-control.

Patient and strong-willed

As a general rule, an intrapreneur will *never* give up as long as they believe that a change will lead to something that is better than whatever is currently in place. This means that they may continue to believe that success is possible and work accordingly long after everyone else has given up. Intrapreneurs use a variety of creative methods to deal with opposition and usually succeed in finding their way past various obstacles and convincing others of what needs to be done.

People around them may feel that the intrapreneur pushes matters too far when they should give up or amend their timescale. They may also see them as too stubborn for their own good.

Visionary

Intrapreneurs see the whole picture and are able to formulate ambitious – sometimes grandiose – visions and goals. They are driven by wanting to accomplish more than is expected of them, and work on the assumption that they are seeking the best possible outcome. They like to do things that no-one has done before and inspire and challenge their co-workers by vividly describing their destination.

People around them may feel that intrapreneurs suffer from delusions of grandeur, lack humility and are unaware of their limitations.

Humble

Intrapreneurs are rarely driven by external factors such as recognition and reward, although they may appreciate sharing these with their team. They do not take the credit for innovations themselves, but will share the honour with

their colleagues and co-workers. While many of them are not aware that they are intrapreneurs themselves, they can spot intrapreneurial characteristics in other people.

People around them may feel that the intrapreneur lacks self-belief or that they do not have the drive and/or ability to compete with other people.

These are several examples of qualities and behaviours that, while natural for many intrapreneurs, can be interpreted in different ways by the people around them. What I see as contradictory in this is that the same person has personal qualities and behaviours that seem from the outside to be mutually opposed. For example, intrapreneurs will exercise firm control but are not keen on planning, and they can be both flexible and focused at the same time. They sell their vision by constantly telling others about it, and get information by consciously listening. As a visionary, they see the whole picture but they are also careful to ensure there is structure and quality in the detail. Intrapreneurs are also very strong-willed and driven but very patient, and they can be both self-confident and humble.

These examples clearly show how this kind of person can make great demands on the people around them just because of the way they are. The same intrapreneur may flourish and innovate successfully in one organisation and feel misunderstood and constrained in another.

My aim is to create a greater understanding of, and knowledge about, similarities and differences to make it easier for co-workers to communicate with each other and work together. I hope that this additional knowledge will reduce the frustration and irritation of co-workers and also create a better environment for the intrapreneur's pursuit of innovation. Of course, it is not just personal qualities and drive that affect an intrapreneur's ability to innovate; there are many more factors that come into play. Additional influences include creativity, motivation and the work environment, colleagues and co-workers and, not least, management. I cover these various areas in the next section.

CHAPTER 2

INFLUENCING THE ABILITY TO INNOVATE

There are many factors affecting a business's overall ability to innovate, and the importance of intrapreneurship and the role of the intrapreneur are issues that form part of a broader context. There has been a discussion for many years about the role of creativity and motivation in work on innovation for both the individual and the team. In addition, research is being carried out into the importance for innovative organisations of leadership and the work environment. Over the years, findings from neurological research have also become a more and more significant element in the debate.

What makes the subject of innovative ability so interesting is the fact that researchers are approaching it from several different angles. Innovation-related research is being pursued in several different areas, including psychology, organisational theory, business administration and economics, and neuroscience. This is resulting in a multitude of theories and conclusions that are also very diverse. In other words, there is no definitive answer to the questions of how innovation works or of how best to approach the issue of the innovative ability of individuals or organisations. Attempting to gain an understanding of the various arguments is an exciting challenge, and, like all knowledge, it helps broaden our perspectives.

I have therefore chosen to present some current research that has relevance to innovative ability in a variety of ways. Areas and researchers have been selected for their ability to help complete the jigsaw that shows what is needed for successful innovation. I have focused on providing the broadest possible picture of how intrapreneurs and the organisation as a whole can help to bring about innovation and the factors that may influence the ability to innovate.

Readers may feel, correctly, that I am summarising quite a number of major issues in what are only short sections of text. My aim is to provide you with some ideas and thoughts about issues and thinking that might be relevant and of interest in various spheres, e.g. things that might affect the ability of the intrapreneur, and thus the organisation, to achieve success. There is scope to add to this information through your own in-depth exploration of the areas that seem most intriguing and fruitful

Different types of innovation

Can we really only expect innovation and development to happen in companies and organisations if rule-breaking, risk-taking, creative intrapreneurs with a thirst for freedom are given free rein both in and outside the organisation? Having studied the research, the nearest we get to an answer is probably "Well ...". It all depends on the type of innovation or outcome an organisation is looking for.

The concept of innovation comes from the Latin innova'tio: to renew, bring about something new, and can be defined as a process in which new ideas, behaviours and procedures are established in a society (Nationalencyklopedin/Swedish National Encyclopaedia 2016). Researchers often discuss innovation from different perspectives. One person who has been very influential in determining how we view both entrepreneurs and innovation and the definitions we use is the economist Joseph Schumpeter (1942). Even though it now dates back over seventy years, his theory of innovation and creative destruction is still extremely relevant.

For Schumpeter, entrepreneurial innovations were the crucial element in the industrial revolution. According to Professor Karl Gratzer (2004), Schumpeter sees the entrepreneur as a tool for economic progress, and views the entrepreneur as an economic function rather than an individual. An innovation can be either a new product, a new method of production or a new technology. It might also involve opening up a new market or creating a new organisation out of existing factors of production. By Schumpeter's definition, an entrepreneur is either a person or a group of individuals that creates something new (an innovation). He sees the role of the entrepreneur as time-limited, since what drives the entrepreneur is the monopoly profit that comes out of the invention of something completely new. Once the innovation has spread, it is no longer an innovation, so market equilibrium is restored and the entrepreneur no longer has a function.

"The struggle between the old and the new, what we call 'creative destruction', is a central concern for Schumpeter," says Gratzer. "The role of the entrepreneur is most critical at the start of an innovation chain. That's when there is a need for someone strong enough to swim against the tide".

Schumpeter divides innovation into radical (disruptive) and incremental (stepwise) innovation. He claims that radical innovation leads to a breakdown of existing social structures. He calls this "creative destruction", and believes that this is essential in order to create space for new development and new knowledge. The consequence of creative destruction is that existing knowledge and structures become less valuable due to new knowledge and structures being developed.

It is precisely because this involves fundamental change, whereby existing structures and behaviours are broken down and/or replaced, that the value of "old" knowledge diminishes. This, in turn, may mean that those who have the old knowledge but not the new feel increasingly insecure.

In summary, Schumpeter divides innovation into:

Incremental, stepwise innovation
' Small changes that gradually reinforce earlier knowledge
' Simplifies functions but does not change human behaviour and is not groundbreaking

Radical, disruptive innovation
' Produces fundamental changes in function, activity and behaviours
' Leads to creative, disruptive change that breaks down and/or replaces existing structures

It is not always easy to see where the line is drawn between the two different types of innovation. The telephone was once a radical innovation, because it profoundly changed the way we communicate. A more recent example is the introduction of email, which, over a few short years in the 1990s, replaced traditional postal mail and which has subsequently also partly replaced the need for ordinary telephone calls. Email has also influenced the way we communicate and helped to dramatically increase our demand for, and expectation of, speed and accessibility. Similarly, smart mobiles and the development of social media have brought about a revolution in our behaviour. Services such as Skype, Facebook, Twitter and Instagram have quickly become new communication channels, which have further shrunk the market for phone calls and letters. Deciding to install cameras in mobiles was an incremental innovation, as we already had access to both cameras and mobiles separately.

Researchers divide intrapreneurs into either independent or management-supported intrapreneurs, and say that they are different in the way they drive innovation. They claim that only the relatively few independent intrapreneurs can create both radical and incremental innovation, while the others drive incremental innovation only. As we will see in the next section, certain factors in the work environment may contribute to incremental innovation and obstruct radical innovation at the same time.

The importance of the work climate for creativity and innovation

Göran Ekvall, a professor emeritus in organisational psychology, links the extent of an organisation's creativity and innovative ability to its prevailing work climate. It was Ekvall who coined the phrase "work climate", after he had spent some time looking at why some co-workers engaged with the organisation they worked for and came up with suggestions and ideas for new solutions while others were not interested at all.

Ekvall (1990) studied various attitudes and behaviours that affect what happens in the workplace. His results led him to draw up a number of factors that need to be in place to stimulate employees' problem-solving ability and creativity. He defines the work climate as the "behaviours, attitudes, feelings and frame of mind of employees in their workplace". The work climate in turn influences operational processes in terms of communication, problem-solving, decision-making and learning. Every individual reacts to the local work climate in different ways.

In Ekvall's opinion (1997), it is difficult to create a specific climate particularly to promote creativity, even though it *is* possible to establish a work climate that favours certain types of innovation. This is because the resources in the workplace, the employees and their knowledge are "filtered" through the organisational climate. It is the extent to which business is centralised and formalised that determines how much creativity is available. The more centralisation and formalisation there is, the lower the level of creativity.

Ekvall divides creativity into two levels, which apply irrespective of whether viewed from the perspective of the product, the individual or the process. He calls one of these levels confirmatory and adaptive creativity and the other radical and innovative creativity. Ekvall says that it is the work climate that determines which of the two different types of creative actions take place within an organisation.

He identifies adaptive co-workers as problem-solvers. These are people that accept given targets and frameworks, seek solutions within a familiar context and try to improve what already exists. Their work brings about small changes that reinforce existing expertise within an organisation. Adaptive innovation simplifies functions but does not change human behaviour and is not groundbreaking in any other way.

For Ekvall, innovators are people who, on encountering a problem, attempt to rephrase it and seek out new solutions from differing points of view. This leads to fundamental changes not only in functions but also in activities and behaviours within organisations or sectors. Innovators will not be contained by a given framework and will explore new pathways rather than improve what already exists. The outcome of an innovator's creative way of working is similar to that of Schumpeter's radical, disruptive innovation.

Ekvall (1997) shows that a particularly radical, innovative creativity requires long-term perspectives and financial resources. This in turn demands a high level of performance in terms of day-to-day operations, which itself hinders creativity. There are some additional obstacles, particularly when it comes to creating the right conditions for radical creativity. Common problems are time pressure, a rapid pace of work and stress in the workplace, circumstances that themselves hamper any type of creativity. A further problem, he claims, is that organisations today – and this includes their standards, systems and procedures – allow innovation by means of adaptive creativity but not by means of radical creativity.

Finally, there is a problematic area of conflict, in that radical innovation places greater demands on the coordination of resources and cooperation between businesses. As increased coordination and control may obstruct creativity, there is an adverse effect on the ability to innovate radically.

Both types of innovation are based on the premise that a change initiative comes from below, not top-down from senior management. Ekvall (DN 2007) says that managers' leadership styles, i.e. how managers address and treat their co-workers, are the key factor in the work climate. He notes that leadership style is responsible for as much as 50% of the difference in the work climate between separate departments in the same company.

Ekvall (1990) feels that there are a number of factors that contribute to a creative environment within an organisation and that they are essential for stimulating the problem-solving ability and creativity of employees. The following is his summary of what he feels are the characteristics of a creative workplace with an innovative work climate:

The first factor is **"challenge and involvement"**. Co-workers feel a commitment to their work, derive enjoyment from it, find it meaningful and feel involved in both day-to-day operations and long-term goals. Creative co-workers are motivated, share ideas and values and feel that they have a contribution to make, which means that they are keen to be involved in developing the business.

"Freedom" is just as important – the freedom for co-workers to think freely, try out new things and take the initiative, and the freedom to talk things over with whoever they want. In creative workplaces, co-workers assume a great deal of individual responsibility, are independent and are encouraged to take the initiative. Ekvall feels that many companies have a kind of "idea-killing mentality". Their first instinct is to find out what the problems are rather than looking at the merits of the idea. Underlying this is a fear of change or a feeling of being threatened.

It is very important for a workplace to have a **low level of conflict**, completely free of, or with only very little, personal conflict or emotional tension. Conflict can quickly lead to deadlock and destroy the creativity in an organisation, and so co-workers need to conduct themselves in a mature manner and be able to deal with differences.

The workplace must offer **"idea-support"**, as it is important that new ideas and suggestions are noted and initiatives are encouraged by management and colleagues in a constructive and positive atmosphere.

The atmosphere will be one of **"trust and openness"**, emotional safety in workplace relationships. Direct, open communication means that co-workers feel safe to adopt new ways of thinking and put forward their ideas and that they will be able to count on individual support, honest treatment and respect. Even if an idea is less good, it will not be shot down or scoffed at – anything is allowed, including mistakes.

"**Liveliness**" is also a factor, as a constant switching between different lines of thought, both positive and negative, assists creativity. A dynamic workplace often operates at high speed and is full of activity. Another factor is "**playfulness and humour**", ensuring that people have fun at work in a relaxed atmosphere with plenty of room for mad ideas and much good-natured joking and laughter.

Ekvall recommends open "**debate and dialogue**". By this he means meetings and discussions with multiple different viewpoints, ideas and perspectives, and a variety of experiences and knowledge. Everyone feels able to express their own opinions and challenge other people's thinking, and all kinds of ideas, both good and bad, are taken on board and undergo intense debate. Tensions and conflict are allowed, but establishing a creative climate requires the right level of tension. The level needs to be high if it is to provide positive tension for the "debate" factor and as low as possible for the "low level of conflict" factor (Isaksen & Ekvall 2010).

The extent of **risk-taking** can determine whether an organisation is creative or stagnating. In a creative work environment, people feel able to test out new ideas and make swift decisions while uncertainty and ambiguity are tolerated. It is OK to fail, and employees launch daring initiatives and are willing to test things out even though there is no certainty about the outcome. People prefer to try out new ideas rather than investigate them.

Finally, good ideas require time, "**idea-time**", to provide opportunities to reflect and monitor the organisation's undertakings – time that can also be used to elaborate new ideas and debates and to create something new.

For Ekvall, the more of the above-mentioned factors that are provided by the workplace, the greater the organisation's ability to innovate. He is of the opinion that the biggest difference between innovative and stagnating companies is the propensity to take risks. In a stagnating organisational climate, individuals are not encouraged to take on challenges or take an active role, and there is no interest in innovation and new ideas. In such organisations, people find it difficult to fulfil their duties, there is no open debate and there is an atmosphere of mistrust and conflict. Ekvall (2000) also feels that, for many companies, a lack of idea-time coupled with strictly-controlled processes such as just-in-time methodology and short lead times keep creativity at a low level.

One problem he describes is that a work climate that promotes a particular type of creativity may make the other type of creativity more difficult, because the various factors affect the work climate in different ways. It is primarily the degree of freedom, liveliness, debate and risk-taking that is the distinguishing factor between a creative work climate that supports radical innovation and one that supports adaptive innovation.

For Ekvall, it is the level of creativity that determines whether or not there is innovation in a workplace at all. He covers the whole range of change-related work, from simple everyday improvements to radical, disruptive innovations. Ekvall's perspective on creativity is thus broader than that of other researchers when innovation and intrapreneurship are being defined, as they do not include minor improvements in their definitions.

It is precisely that broader thinking that makes Ekvall interesting. He identifies a range of different factors that he claims contribute to a creative work climate and also states that it is the level of creativity that determines the type of change or innovation in any organisation. This means that *any* type of change is governed by Ekvall's factors, which are in principle the same factors identified by other researchers as necessary for intrapreneurs and intrapreneurial activity.

Factors such as challenge and involvement, freedom, a low level of conflict, idea-support, trust and openness, playfulness and humour, debate and dialogue, risk-taking and idea-time are all essential if entrepreneurs are to innovate successfully. This was made very clear in the interview with P in the previous section. At the same time, Ekvall shows that a work climate of this sort has benefits for intrapreneurs and other co-workers alike, because, fundamentally, the issue is whether an individual needs to feel motivated to be able to perform well in the workplace. This will be the subject of the next chapter.

Motivation leads to creativity

During the course of the 20th century, several theories were put forward on the subject of what motivates people, how they are motivated, and why some people appear motivated while others seem to have no motivation at all.

One of the best-known researchers on the subject of motivation is the American psychologist Abraham Maslow. In 1943, he introduced a model illustrating a human being's needs and how they are prioritised. Maslow was interested in what it means to be in good mental health. He believed that the most important role of therapy was to remove the barriers preventing people from growing and maturing.

Maslow (1954) divided human needs into different groups and ranked them in a five-tier hierarchy of needs. At the bottom are the **Physiological needs** (food, drink, sleep, reproduction, avoidance of pain), followed by the need for **Safety** (security, order, stability), and for **Love/Belonging** (family, relations, love, friendship). At the top are the need for **Esteem** (self-esteem, competence, the respect of others, independence, status) and for **Self-Actualization** (morality, creativity, freedom from prejudice).

In Maslow's view, the lower levels give rise to *deficiency motivation* and so these needs must be met before other needs can be prioritised. Various life events can cause a person to move between the different levels of need, and, in a crisis, someone might slide down the scale and have to start from scratch. By contrast, the fifth state, Self-Actualization, will cause *growth motivation,* and is a state that is only created when other needs have been satisfied. Only then will an individual have the inner freedom to give expression to the creative talents inherent in their personality. Maslow calls the satisfaction of basic needs "*coping*" and the satisfaction of self-actualization needs "*expressive behaviour*".

Maslow believes that before an individual can develop motivation, they need space to develop their cognitive ability. This requires certain conditions to be met, for example the freedom to think, seek information, express oneself and do what one likes, provided no harm is done to anyone else. Having an understanding of what is happening in the world around you is a fundamental human need, and the urge to seek out new knowledge and to learn stays with us throughout our lives. According to research, it is the individual's motivation that leads to creativity. Since Maslow, many well-known researchers have put forward theories on motivation suggesting that it is an individual's motivation that leads to creativity.

One of the best-established theories on motivation, *The Self-Determination Theory* (SDT), was developed by professors of psychology Edward L. Deci and Richard M. Ryan (1985, 2000). They claim that motivation is developed internally and is based on fundamental human needs, because humans are naturally curious, enquiring, adventurous and self-motivating. People are driven by having the opportunity to develop their skills and abilities, take the initiative and feel an affiliation with other people and their surroundings. SDT says that people are most committed and creative when they feel that they are acting of their own free will and working towards targets that they perceive as meaningful.

Deci and Ryan (2000) concluded that individuals are driven either by intrinsic or extrinsic motivation, and sometimes by both. Intrinsic motivation is described as arising spontaneously and as something that cannot be forced. It is associated with internal stimuli, such as personal interest, pleasure or a sense of meaningfulness. If people are motivated by intrinsic motivation, it is easier to learn new things and assimilate ideas, which is why it is primarily intrinsic motivation that leads to creativity in the workplace. In turn, extrinsic motivation is based on external stimuli, perhaps a good reputation, status or financial reward. Extrinsic motivation can be associated with feelings such as "I should" and "I must". According to research, individuals who are driven only by extrinsic motivation find it more difficult to learn new things and develop a lower level of creativity.

In the SDT model, the degree of intrinsic motivation is influenced by three factors:

1. **Competence:** Striving for continuous development and for relevant feedback from people around you

2. **Autonomy:** A sense of being able to act of your own free will and influence your own situation

3. **Relatedness:** Experiencing meaningful, supportive social relationships and pleasure in engaging and contributing to something greater than yourself

The SDT model became more widely known when the author Daniel H.

Pink (2009) used it as the basis of his popular science book *Drive: The Surprising Truth About What Motivates Us.* Pink questions why increasing numbers of employees are leaving their jobs to start their own businesses. He notes that people are primarily driven by intrinsic motivation, and argues against industry's use of older models based on extrinsic motivation, such as financial reward and fear of punishment. Pink feels that extrinsic factors only come into play when the tasks being undertaken are simple ones. By contrast, extrinsic rewards frustrate work that requires cognitive skills, decision-making or creativity because they distract focus from the task in hand. He concludes that companies need to invest in supporting the intrinsic motivation of their staff by allowing them to be autonomous, providing opportunities for them to achieve mastery [through continuous personal development] and providing a meaningful purpose. If they do not, more and more employees will leave their jobs.

It is interesting to consider the SDT motivation model in relation to the intrapreneurial personality. The model supports the idea that the intrapreneur is a person who:

- does not want to stagnate
- takes a holistic approach
- is strongly motivated
- is able to work in a situation of great uncertainty
- takes risks and can see opportunities
- has great confidence in their own abilities
- is creative whatever their motivation (intrinsic/extrinsic or both)

Where this interpretation differs from what we have noted previously in this book is in the supposition that the intrapreneur is creative irrespective of motivation. Pinchot and others claim that it is the vision, together with the dreams, freedom, challenges and personal development, i.e. the intrinsic motivation, that drives the intrapreneur. Researchers Marylene Gagné and Edward L. Deci (2005) believe that an intrapreneur is creative whatever the circumstances.

The concept of creativity itself is one that is of great interest to researchers, and there are often links to different types of motivation. In 2010, researchers Teresa M. Amabile and Beth A. Hennessey identified and summarised various different theories about creativity that have been introduced by various researchers in recent decades. Their report, *Creativity*, describes the research on this topic and what supports or obstructs the creative process. The report demonstrates that interest in research on creativity has risen sharply in recent years, but also that researchers are less and less in agreement. Amabile and Hennessey say that the main reason for this is that the researchers are not aware of findings in each other's areas.

Their report therefore recommends more cross-disciplinary research and recognises the great potential of areas such as neurological research, with the aim of identifying connections between creativity and various brain functions. They also report some of the conclusions from their summary and state that, taken as a whole, the research shows that:

' Creative individuals are better at dealing with set-backs and problems than others

' The degree of creativity is dependent on
  . how motivated the individual is to find solutions
  . the individual's knowledge of the area in question
  . the individual's knowledge of creative processes

' An individual's motivation may be
  . high or low
  . intrinsic or extrinsic

' Individuals driven by intrinsic motivation are more likely to act in an intrapreneurial way than those driven by extrinsic motivation

Intrapreneurs are driven by intrinsic motivation

Researchers now agree that people are more creative, productive and committed, and work better together, if they are driven by intrinsic motivation. Teresa Amabile looked further into how motivation works at the level of the individual. Working with Steven Kramer (2011), she studied 12,000 diary entries that had been made by selected co-workers over a certain period. The study involves 238 people working on important innovatory projects in various different companies, and the researchers look in detail at what is motivating them. It is based partly on co-workers' own comments about their tasks, including how they see the manager's role in the project, and partly on responses from the managers themselves.

Amabile and other researchers have previously established that managers have an important role in strengthening co-workers' intrinsic motivation. Their role includes setting **clear goals**, providing **interpersonal support**, ensuring every co-worker gets **recognition** for their various efforts and **minimising daily hassles**. However, their work on the diary entries led Amabile and Kramer to realise that there is something even more important that has not yet been fully recognised. They say that only when co-workers feel that their work is **meaningful** and that they **make progress in the work** will their need for intrinsic motivation be fulfilled (Amabile and Kramer talk of a person's "inner work life").

Amabile and Kramer's investigations show that most managers do not realise the importance of meaningful tasks and making progress for intrinsic motivation. As part of the study, managers at all levels are asked how important they feel five different motivators are for their co-workers: incentives, recognition, clear goals, interpersonal support and meaningful progress in their work. Only 8 per cent of the 669 senior executives participating in the study rank progress as the most important motivator. The researchers note that if they had chosen randomly, 20 per cent of them would have chosen this as the most important factor for intrinsic motivation.

Instead, the diary entries reveal that managers at all levels regularly, and unintentionally, undermine creativity, productivity, and commitment. Their everyday words and actions have an adverse effect on the meaningfulness of the work, making it less likely that their co-workers will experience a sense of intrinsic motivation.

The co-workers taking part in Amabile and Kramer's study are, as has been mentioned, innovative people in innovative organisations. I draw from this that the study involves a large number of intrapreneurs, which makes it particularly interesting from my point of view. The researchers highlight examples of situations in which co-workers' intrinsic motivation is adversely affected by the unconscious attitudes and behaviours of their immediate manager. Such situations might include dismissing the importance of co-workers' work or ideas or destroying the sense of ownership by moving people off project teams before a task is complete. Or altering the goals so often that people despair of their work ever being finished. Or failing to keep co-workers up to date on important changes and customer priorities.

In addition to situations involving co-workers and their immediate managers, there are also traps that senior managers and top management can easily fall into. Even if there are only a few sets of circumstances in which management can directly influence the situation of co-workers, their actions can nevertheless have devastating consequences for co-workers' commitment and sense of meaningfulness. However, Amabile and Kramer (2012) make it clear that these traps can be avoided.

The following are four examples of traps that senior managers and top management might fall into:

Signalling that mediocrity is OK

Many companies have a clear vision revolving around the achievement of lofty goals. However, there is a danger that the words and actions of top management may inadvertently signal the opposite. The researchers give the example of a new top-management team embracing an ambitious vision that proposes to prioritise innovation by setting up entrepreneurial, cross-functional business teams. The intention, in theory, is for the teams to work autonomously and to manage their portion of the company's resources to invest independently in product innovation. In the annual report, there is a statement from senior management saying how important they feel innovation is for the company. In practice, however, top management is so focused on keeping costs down that they repeatedly disregard the teams' supposed autonomy and impose compulsory cost savings targets.

As a result, the development of new products comes to a halt and cost savings have a negative impact on the quality of existing products. Co-workers feel that the company is starting to lose its market lead because it contents itself with mediocre products. This in turn means they lose pride in their work, resulting in a sharp decrease in intrinsic motivation. In the study, the researchers note that many co-workers become disengaged and the best of them leave the company. They also give other examples of how senior management may proclaim their company's ability to innovate externally while in practice delaying projects and processes because they are uncomfortable with risk-taking and responsibility.

Having an erratic strategy

Amabile and Kramer have a name for the situation in which senior management spends excessive time and energy on everything that is happening in their external environment – they call it *"strategic attention deficit disorder"*. It means that they allow far too many new ideas, trends and other external factors to influence company strategy, resulting in constantly changing priorities. Sometimes the unpredictability is due to internal disputes about priorities amongst top management. This can mean that projects are both started and abandoned rapidly with no time spent on evaluation. This often happens without the co-workers being told the reasons for the changes, making it difficult for them to set their own priorities. If top management itself is not clear about exactly where the company is heading, co-workers will find it very difficult to maintain a strong sense of intrinsic motivation.

Incompetent, uncoordinated leadership

The researchers found that many managers believe that their businesses are operating smoothly and are unaware of the things that are not working. Oblivious to the consequences, top management may contribute to what can be a farcical situation either through its actions or by failing to act. It might be that management sets the wrong priorities, and demands overly complex matrix reporting structures or solutions that do not work in practice. Alternatively, top management may be indecisive or avoid dealing with awkward situations, such as failing to hold support functions accountable for coordinated action. When there are no coordinating and support functions in an organisation, or they do not work, co-workers stop believing that they can produce something of high quality. That makes it very difficult for them to retain their intrinsic motivation.

Setting over-ambitious, unattainable goals

Finally, the researchers warn about the dangers of top management setting highly ambitious goals. Sometimes it makes sense for management to formulate a bold vision and powerful strategies that appeal to co-workers' emotions and values. Some companies do not succeed in this, and it is often because they have devised goals that are either so extreme that they seem unattainable or so vague that they feel meaningless. Co-workers find it difficult to engage when the goals bear absolutely no relation to their reality. When goals are meaningless, co-workers may find themselves in a vacuum where they become cynical and disengaged, losing their intrinsic motivation as a result.

Amabile and Kramer give tips to senior managers about how they can ensure their co-workers gain a sense of meaningfulness and intrinsic motivation. They say that it is management that is best placed to identify, and maintain an overview of, the purpose of the work that co-workers do in the organisation. This means they have the ability to clarify the business's objectives and provide consistent support through their actions. This can be done, for example, by being consistent when communicating with co-workers and employing strategies compatible with the organisation's capabilities. It also means having an understanding of how and where communication is of most use.

In order to understand the perspective of the individual co-worker, it is sensible for those in management and leadership positions to refer to their own experience before asking their co-workers to undertake a specific task. They should ask themselves to what extent they would have perceived the situation as engaging and meaningful. The researchers also emphasise the importance of early-warning systems that can indicate when the view from the top does not match the reality on the ground. They can also make managers aware of when procedures and processes take up too much of their co-workers' time so that they no longer feel that their work has meaning.

Amabile and Kramer's descriptions of poor leadership may seem stereotypical, but they do provide clear warning signals and show what the effect of managers' unconscious behaviour can be. According to the researchers, managers will normally exhibit a range of behaviours in the workplace, and while some of them may be less desirable than others, they may not all affect the motivation of co-workers in the same way.

Amabile and Kramer's study of creativity has a natural focus on managerial shortcomings, but, as Ekvall's research has previously made clear, it is not only the managers that influence the creative climate in a workplace. So it is important to note that the lack of awareness of both managers and co-workers about their own behaviour and how they affect the people around them is one of the main factors affecting a business's ability to innovate.

The intrapreneurial team

There was discussion amongst researchers at an early stage as to whether intrapreneurship required an individual intrapreneur or whether an entire working group could develop intrapreneurship together. Pinchot and Pellman's (1999) view was that "The best teams are cross-functional or cross-disciplinary. Most teams are led by one intrapreneur, but all the members of the team can be called intrapreneurs as long as each understands the whole dream and is continually working to find better ways to make it happen."

For Pinchot (1985), the intrapreneur themselves recruits a cross-functional project team that gradually develops into an intrapreneurial team. Both the intrapreneur and the team need support from one or more people at a high level in the organisation. This might be a "sponsor", who removes any organisational, political or financial obstacles – perhaps the CEO, the owner or a previous intrapreneur. Alternatively, the team might be supported by a "protector", i.e. someone in the senior management team who is open to new ideas. The protector accepts and encourages change and allows the team a good deal of freedom so that they can carry out the project in their own way.

The members of the intrapreneurial team focus on the needs of the project and identify with the new project rather than with an individual function. An intrapreneurial team will often bring together people with a broad range of skills, from product development and finance to marketing and sales. In the interviews, several of the intrapreneurs asserted that the team is the key to success; in fact, there is general agreement that, without a functioning team, there can be no innovation. It is usually the intrapreneur themselves who selects the team, possibly with guidance from someone high up in the organisation. The intrapreneurs say that the members of their teams appreciate the opportunity to work together with other knowledgeable colleagues and also to share in the intrapreneur's vision, inspiration and concrete ideas. They also believe that it is common for the intrapreneur to push themselves hard, thus becoming a role model for the team. Their co-workers in turn respond by also working particularly hard and in a very focused way, with a degree of commitment that then stimulates yet more motivation and creativity.

When the intrapreneurs describe the most important success factors, they often talk of the "personal chemistry" between colleagues or team members. The concept sums up their view of how the intrapreneurial team works, and includes the team members' attitudes towards each other, mutual respect, shared values, the right combination of expertise, and consensus on the vision and aims: in other words, those aspects that they all agree are the basis of the trust and open communication that must exist within the team. After it has been working together for a while, the team normally develops its own culture, which allows for open dialogue without personal criticism or negativity. The team members' positive attitude gradually evolves, enhancing motivation and creativity and increasing the energy in the group.

Intrapreneurs see their most important task as inspiring the team and conceptualising the vision. That includes situations where the team has a significant workload or is experiencing set-backs. Several intrapreneurs describe how they strive to protect the team from negative external influences. As the team's efforts bring success and acclaim, the intrapreneur's importance for the climate in the group declines. At that stage, the team members start to be driven by their own internal motivation and to motivate themselves and each other to an even greater degree.

A feature that intrapreneur-driven projects have in common is that the workload for both the intrapreneur and the team is often extreme. The intrapreneur is often the project leader and responsible for reporting to management, which adds an additional dimension to their work, and in addition to that, most intrapreneurs usually also have an operational role that has its own demands over and above the project work. Time for reflection, feeding back and developing new ideas is often hard to come by. This can have a negative impact on the team, as the members need to be kept supplied with energy and inspiration – because however good the personal chemistry between the intrapreneur and the team, the team is dependent on outside support. All team members depend on support from senior managers in their organisation in order to develop and retain their internal motivation.

There are varying views as to when and how support should be sought and which manager should be approached. More established intrapreneurs will have built up a reservoir of trust with management and will therefore be able to work relatively freely without any direct demands. Others need to perform a balancing act, as too much attention from managers can also increase expectations of rapid success. One intrapreneur put it as follows: "We need time to experiment on a small scale before we should be required to present a finished prototype or beta version. Sometimes the manager can be very eager ..." The response suggests that even a sponsor or a protector as defined by Pinchot may, with the best of intentions, push the team a little too quickly or too hard, which can make innovatory work more difficult.

The importance of colleagues and the rest of the organization

As both research and the experiences of myself and others show, co-workers and colleagues are important factors in the extent to which the intrapreneur and the intrapreneurial team will be successful. Because intrapreneurs have an ability to surround themselves with the skills that are needed, it is seldom expertise or resources that are the biggest barrier to success, at least not in the short term.

Several intrapreneurs noted that they had had success "in spite of management and the rest of the organisation, rather than because of them", and that they perceived their organisation in general as unwieldy and slow-moving. New ideas and visions do not always meet with a positive response, and may be seen as somewhat odd or even provocative and unnecessary.

The intrapreneurs claim that middle-level managers in particular clearly show that they see work on innovation as a disturbance. It is something that diverts resources away from them rather than an inspiring challenge. The intrapreneurs take this to mean that the managers are focused on day-to-day operations and are worried that they may be held to account if they do not prioritise their own targets. The most negative reactions come from the managers who have not been kept informed by their superiors or who have not had any training on or information about the project before it started.

There is sometimes envy from colleagues who have not been chosen to take part in the project. This is particularly apparent in cases where the intrapreneurial team eventually achieves success, and the positive atmosphere in the team and its accomplishments start to attract attention externally. Significant cultural differences or different climates within and outside the team can also be a source of frustration and envy. Several intrapreneurs say that the attitude of one or a small number of colleagues can be crucial in terms of whether or not a project is successful. This is particularly apparent in cases where the intrapreneur does not have a sponsor or protector at management level, leaving the field wide open for negative comments and actions.

On the other hand, virtually all the intrapreneurs highlight collaboration with colleagues outside the team – cross-functional collaboration – as one of the key success factors. The collaboration leads to an exchange of skills and a broadening of expertise and resources, in turn facilitating the identification of new opportunities and solutions. It is also quite common for the intrapreneur to initiate various types of training, both for the members of the intrapreneurial team and for colleagues in the rest of the organisation. This is seen as a means for the intrapreneur to share their own picture of the situation and the vision that is the point of departure for the project. Discussion and training on the organisation's values and goals are also important. It is helpful for the intrapreneur if there is already a shared view in the organisation to lean on, as this can make it easier to achieve greater understanding and greater acceptance for the link to their own vision.

Management is the key to intrapreneurial success

The importance of management and leadership for the work climate and the effectiveness and motivation of co-workers has long been a focus of interest for researchers. A number of different leadership theories have been put forward over the years. As mentioned earlier, several of them focus on the importance of leadership for creativity and the capacity for innovation.

A lack of knowledge, fear or stress on the part of either managers or co-workers can be major factors in a negative work climate. In critical situations, there is a tendency to focus on the manager's lack of leadership. It is important, therefore, to report both what the intrapreneurs say when interviewed and what research has to tell us about the importance of leadership for an organisation's success. We then in turn need to explain how the latter relates to intrapreneurship and the ability to innovate.

Several of the intrapreneurs interviewed say that, to start with at least, they often work on development projects on their own initiative, within the context of their normal duties. This means it can take some time before the projects are known about and, hopefully, approved at management level. They conclude that, in the long run, projects cannot survive without active support and encouragement from management. Experience tells them that, sooner or later, projects with no support will fail.

Research confirms that intrapreneurs like to work in an unconventional way within an organisation and sometimes break existing structures. It is therefore important to have some sort of bridge to those with overall responsibility for the organisation to avoid projects failing. Management, or at least parts of it, need to be able to feel that they can put their trust in the intrapreneur as an individual and have confidence in their ideas and vision. This is essential to ensure the intrapreneur gets the space they need to do their job and important for reducing any feelings of insecurity on the part of management. The safer they feel with the intrapreneur as an individual, the more they will be willing to give that person the freedom to test different options while allowing for some risk-taking.

The interviews tell us that the more success an intrapreneur has over time, the easier it becomes for them to persuade others to believe in their continued success and the less time needs to be spent on presenting ideas internally. The dilemma they face is that things sometimes have to go wrong in order for the outcomes to be really first class, and in the meantime mutual trust must be maintained even in the event of set-backs. If not, expectations of constant success can become a burden on the intrapreneur. There will be less insecurity if management ensures that the organisation has a clear rooted vision and explicit, shared goals. This will provide some reassurance for all involved, even if they are not always in agreement about, or do not always accept, the route to achieving the goals.

It is not uncommon for intrapreneurs, at least during their first projects, to work initially in secret and then to move on to quietly testing out their ideas. Some of those I interviewed call this "working under the radar". The intrapreneur feels so strongly about what needs to be done that their conviction takes over, even if they run the risk of strong opposition both from management and the rest of the organisation when their activity becomes known. This is firmly backed up by research showing that about half of the intrapreneurs who have implemented major changes have encountered considerable opposition from management and/or the rest of the organisation in relation to their innovatory work (Bosma et al. 2012).

When a development project is a success, management normally recognises the intrapreneur's achievements within the organisation – even if the intrapreneur's creative, innovatory thinking and intrapreneurial ability are not always rewarded and the focus is more on the positive financial outcome of the project. Unfortunately, there are also examples of cases, although only a few, where management takes the credit for major innovatory successes itself. Consciously or unconsciously, the intrapreneur is completely side-lined, which effectively diminishes their internal motivation to continue developing.

The interviews make it clear that there are major differences between the situation of the intrapreneur recruited direct by the company's CEO or a high-ranking manager and that of the intrapreneur "inherited" by an incoming manager. This is particularly noticeable where the intrapreneur had a clear intrapreneurial role in the organisation at the point when the new manager came into post. Intrapreneurs that are either recruited personally by the CEO, are sought out and approached about a particular project or have a good connection with management in some other way have an excellent starting point for their work. They then have both the "sponsor" and the "protector" that Pinchot (1985) says are essential if an intrapreneur is to be successful.

Several of the intrapreneurs, who had experience of both personal recruitment and later being inherited by a new manager, describe how they felt they were a threat to the incoming manager. The reasons for this vary. In some cases, the new manager had a completely different personality and a different focus, which meant that they did not see anything of direct value in the intrapreneur's work. In others, the new manager was uncomfortable with the intrapreneur's broad knowledge of the overall picture and the challenges faced by the organisation and their clear ideas about what needed to be done. Whatever the reason, in such situations the intrapreneur is in danger of being left out in the cold, often without knowing what is happening. There can be additional complications if the new manager is appointed with instructions to reduce costs and make efficiency savings. The personal qualities that a manager employs to implement efficiency measures and short-term performance targets differ markedly from those of the intrapreneur. Since an intraprencur operates through the use of the organisation's resources, it is important that they have access to their own budget and can work autonomously with a long-term perspective. A new manager that introduces restrictions can, often unconsciously, but quickly and very easily, destroy the entire innovatory and intrapreneurial climate of the workplace.

Any conflicts of interest of this sort will be very apparent out in the organisation. Removing or severely restricting an intrapreneur's opportunities to innovate risks killing off their spirit of initiative and innovation, and that of the other co-workers too, for a long time to come. The way the intrapreneur is treated is critical to the organisation's future development, as the rest of the organisation will notice what happens when someone dares to operate outside the box. To avoid this situation, even the most imaginative of employees may find that the simplest course of action is either to adopt a passive, risk-free stance or to leave the organisation.

Successful and credible leadership

Because the qualities and motivations of intrapreneurs differ from those of other employees, it might be thought that they need a different type of leadership to their colleagues and co-workers. They obviously do require something other than normal leadership if they are to drive innovation. However, the general characteristics of successful and credible leadership identified by the well-known leadership researchers Jim Kouzes and Barry Posner are not very different from those of the leadership needed by an intrapreneur.

Kouzes and Posner undertake research into individual leadership qualities, and have published several books that have been translated into twenty languages, with several million copies sold. Their books *The Leadership Challenge* (1987) and *The Truth about Leadership* (2010) summarise their research into the characteristics of the most successful and credible leadership.

Their research began thirty years ago when they asked a number of leaders, "What do you actually do when you are at your personal best?" Over the years, they have interviewed thousands of managers and co-workers and accumulated hundreds of thousands of responses to their enquiries. Studying the results of their research, I find that there are clear parallels between successful, credible leadership and the leadership needed for successful intrapreneurship.

Their conclusion is that leadership is something everyone can learn, but that practice is needed to become a good leader. Their findings from the research are the basis of their *"Five Practices of Exemplary Leadership"* model, and they show that those leaders who employ the practices proposed in the model are seen by their co-workers as better leaders. The co-workers are happier with their managers, have a more positive attitude to their work and are more productive than their colleagues. My reading of the practices suggests that they are consistent with effective methods for managing intrapreneurs.

I provide a summary of Kouzes and Posner's practices below, and also reflect on how they can apply to the realities of the intrapreneur.

- **Model the Way**

Leaders are urged to follow their own values while also affirming shared values. They are expected to set an example and to conduct themselves just as they encourage their co-workers to conduct themselves. One way of 'modelling the way' is to use symbolic language such as metaphor, narrative and pictures as aids.

Reflection: Intrapreneurs need a corporate culture that is value-led

Intrapreneurs need to feel that they are going their own way, but they will willingly follow someone they believe in. They are guided by their own vision, which is linked to the organisation's and can only function if they share the organisation's values. Managers can help to create an innovative environment by being open about their own personal values, demonstrating trust in the intrapreneur's ability and tolerating mistakes and failure.

- **Inspire a Shared Vision**

Leaders have responsibility for envisioning the future by visualising possibilities. They must persuade others to share a common picture of the future by attracting them with shared expectations. The vision should be about possibilities, hopes, dreams and ambitions in the very long term, while goals are short term and quantifiable. To share their vision, a leader must both believe in it themselves and act in accordance with it. A leader must also get to know the ambitions, hopes and dreams of their co-workers. The clearer the shared vision, the more productive and committed the co-workers. Kouzes and Posner's research shows that, where there is a shared vision, there is an increase in levels of job satisfaction, motivation, loyalty and pride in the organisation, values become clearer and there is greater team spirit.

Reflection: Allow the intrapreneur to live their vision
An intrapreneur follows their own vision, which is closely linked to that of the organisation. When the manager affirms, recognises and encourages the intrapreneur's initiatives and ideas, they are able to live out their dreams through their work, thus creating an even stronger link between the intrapreneur and the organisation.

- **Challenge the Process**

The leader's task is to encourage co-workers to venture beyond their boundaries. They should challenge existing processes and seek out opportunities to innovate and improve. Leaders do not see mistakes and failures as anything other than an opportunity to learn something new. By establishing a safe climate that allows co-workers to experiment and take risks, leaders and co-workers can together take one step at a time, test new ways of working and learn from their experiences. This will enable co-workers to make greater strides with confidence.

Reflection: Give the intrapreneur support, responsibility and autonomy
Intrapreneurs constantly challenge existing processes and structures and push at boundaries. It is important for managers to show that their intrapreneurial behaviour is accepted, supported and encouraged both by their immediate manager and top management. This implies a culture of openness in which intrapreneurs are not afraid to share their ideas with others. All co-workers should be encouraged to come up with improvements and suggestions for development that go beyond any established <u>solutions</u>. Once ideas have been

put forward, the manager must provide support in the form of advice and resources to speed up development, at the same time allowing space for the intrapreneur to take responsibility for the process themselves.

• Enable Others to Act

The leader's task is to create a safe, trustful environment. This is done by removing obstacles and barriers, so that co-workers are able to do the things they are good at, and by promoting teamwork. Leaders support collaboration by establishing trust, facilitating relationships and increasing the empowerment and skills of co-workers. A leader cannot achieve results alone, and so must demonstrate confidence and interest in their co-workers and allow them to develop their talents, proficiency and self-confidence.

-Reflection: Intrapreneurs need adapted processes and good communication
Intrapreneurship requires a decentralised structure in which the manager delegates as much as possible so that decisions are made by those with the most knowledge and skills. There should be as few restrictive rules and as little bureaucracy as possible. Managers should ensure that they promote an open, cross-functional exchange of ideas within the organisation and encourage the exchange of different types of expertise through external networks. It is a good idea to provide a variety of platforms for the exchanging and testing of ideas – innovation requires both time and resources.

• Encourage the Heart

A leader must recognise and celebrate co-workers' contributions fairly and candidly. It is the leader's responsibility to create a sense of community in which everyone's victories are celebrated, for example by acknowledging co-workers' achievements, whether major or minor, and showing appreciation of their unique skills.

Reflection: Intrapreneurs are driven by intrinsic motivation and incentives
Intrapreneurs are driven by intrinsic motivation and by opportunities to develop their ideas. At the same time, they want to be recognised and acknowledged for their work, preferably along with their teams. Performance-based financial reward is important but not sufficient in itself. It is important that rewards are both short and long term. Intrapreneurs are normally driven by financial incentives, but most are not opposed to a financial reward after

the event (in the form of a bonus or share of profits) – on the contrary, it can be seen as positive from the point of view of 'fairness'. In general, rewards should encourage risk-taking, and some organisations use different types of rewards, such as guaranteeing resources and time for the intrapreneur to undertake other projects.

The practices above represent Kouzes and Posner's conclusions about how successful and credible leadership works in practice, and my reflections show how important they are for successful innovation too.

In their book *The Truth about Leadership* (2010), Kouzes and Posner claim that there has been little change in successful behaviours and habits in the last thirty years, even though the circumstances in which business and leadership operate have changed radically. Based on research into the most successful and credible leadership, they have drawn up ten universal truths about leadership which they say have global validity and operate across generational boundaries.

These "truths" apply both to the leadership needed to drive successful innovation and to the intrapreneur as an individual. The latter is very much in line with Pinchot's view that intrapreneurs must be talented managers if they are to be able to bring other, skilled co-workers along with them. Strong leadership qualities are essential for strengthening the project team and convincing co-workers of the need to adhere to and carry out the intrapreneur's ideas. Positive leadership qualities are also needed to be able to make quick decisions in uncertain circumstances.

The ten truths that Kouzes and Posner say leaders need to address are given here, along with my comments on how they relate to the truths of intrapreneurs themselves.

1. Individuals make a difference

Leaders must believe in themselves. To be a leader, you need to believe that you can have a positive impact on other people. Leadership begins when a leader believes that they can make a difference. For Kouzes and Posner, every individual can make a difference if they are set on changing the status quo.

One of the strongest motivating factors for an intrapreneur is changing the status quo.

2. Credibility is the foundation of leadership

When a leader is believable, people are more likely to have confidence in and willingly follow them, and also provide their time, energy, experience, intelligence, creativity and support. Without credibility, there can be no relationship, and without relationships there is no leadership.

When a leader has a high level of credibility, co-workers' productivity increases and so the leader becomes more effective. In a survey as part of Kouzes and Posner's study, four qualities consistently received an average of over 60 per cent of votes, irrespective of where in the world the question was asked. Co-workers felt that the most important quality of a leader was that they were:

- Honest
- Inspiring   } Credible leader
- Competent
- Forward-looking

For their actions to be credible, leaders must do what they say they will do. This means being so clear about what they believe in that their beliefs can be implemented in practice on a daily basis. A person who consistently lives by their values exhibits honesty and trustworthiness.

> An intrapreneur must be credible in order to bring co-workers (and managers) along with them, and must also be someone with ideas and dreams about the future.

3. Values drive commitment

Effective leaders understand who they are, where they come from, the values that guide them and what drives them. For a leader to be committed to their work, there must be a good fit between what the leader values and what the organisation values.

Leadership is a relationship, and clear values are the key to mutual understanding in that relationship.

> An intrapreneur needs to share the values and vision of the organisation if they are to be able to drive innovation.

4. Focusing on the future sets leaders apart

To have a vision, a leader must have an ability to imagine and communicate exciting future possibilities. Leaders do not think about the here and now; they take a long-term view, work out what might be on the horizon and move forward. Far-sightedness is the main quality that sets leaders apart from individual co-workers. Co-workers expect the leader to know where they are heading and to have an idea of the general direction of travel.

An intrapreneur sees their task as formulating and visualising the future in the form of ideas and carrying through innovations.

5. You can't do it alone

Leadership is a shared responsibility. No leader has ever achieved anything exceptional without the skills and support of other people. Kouzes and Posner say that what strengthens and maintains the relationship between the leader and co-workers is that leaders are obsessed with what is best for other people, not what is best for them. The leader's task is to increase people's sense of empowerment, self-confidence and personal effectiveness. Exemplary leaders ask questions, give support, develop their skills and ask for help. They bring people together for a common purpose and make them feel that anything is possible. They enable others to take responsibility for their own lives and become better people.

An intrapreneur is dependent on the skills and support of other people. They gather people into an intrapreneurial team where they work together for a common purpose, and they make them feel that anything is possible.

6. Trust rules

If a leader cannot do it alone but is dependent on others, what is needed to make things happen? Trust is the social glue that holds individuals and groups together, and it has to be earned. Kouzes and Posner's research shows that the degree of trust co-workers have in leaders determines the amount of influence they have. You have to demonstrate trust before you can receive it.

Research shows that leaders build up trust by:
- Behaving consistently and predictably
- Communicating clearly
- Treating promises seriously
- Being forthright and frank

An intrapreneur and their intrapreneurial team need a work climate with a high degree of trust and confidence to be able to establish the openness and creativity needed for innovation.

7. Challenge is the crucible for greatness

The most admired leaders are those able to lead others through major challenges. Leaders tend to see the opportunity in adversity, and they will take any action needed to go forward. This can be stressful, and the authors remind us that to successfully lead change, leaders must be strong and resilient. Leaders need to believe that they can influence a situation positively through their own efforts.

Leadership is about leading others through challenges and change, and this requires courage, the ability to continue pushing forward and resilience to stress. Also needed are the courage to deal with set-backs and an ability to bounce back when mistakes are made.

An intrapreneur takes risks and drives change in the face of opposition, employing extensive reserves of will-power and patience.

8. Either lead by example or don't lead at all

Credibility is the foundation of leadership, and Kouzes and Posner's research shows that the most credible behaviour is "Do What You Say You Will Do". Seeing is believing, and co-workers need to see the leader living by their own standards and values.

An intrapreneur links their vision and values to those of the organisation, and if top management does not adhere to these values they lose all credibility. If this happens, the intrapreneur will decide not to drive innovation.

9. The best leaders are the best learners

You can learn to be a leader. Leadership is not an inbuilt ability and it can be learned in different ways. The key to becoming a leader is to have a passion for learning. To learn effectively, a leader must be open to new experiences and to getting feedback from people around them – without feedback, it is difficult to get better at leadership. The authors say that learning requires conscious training, time and attention, target-setting, practice, feedback and good coaching.

> An intrapreneur is driven by new knowledge, personal development and the freedom to find new ways of doing things. An intrapreneur both is – and needs – a leader that understands, accepts and supports.

10. Leadership is an affair of the heart

Research shows that high-performing leaders are in touch with their emotions. They are successful because they listen to what their heart tells them and establish close contact with other people. As a result, both the leader and the co-workers are able to engage more deeply with the work. Their focus is on their co-workers rather than on themselves, and they help them grow and develop so that they can become independent.

It is important for leaders to show their co-workers that they care about them. The best way to do this is to work alongside the co-workers, give them positive reinforcement and communicate the vision. Leaders that are visible and accessible are seen as more genuine, approachable and human. Exemplary leaders are positive and optimistic, and create the emotional energy needed for others to achieve success. Kouzes and Posner say that it is the leader's duty to accentuate the positive, not least when times are tough and uncertain.

> An intrapreneur is positive, focuses on opportunities and visualises dreams, and in addition needs a leader who affirms this.

Reading Kouzes and Posner's books, it may seem that it is almost impossible to meet all the requirements and expectations associated with being a successful and exemplary leader. It is encouraging, however, that they claim that anyone can learn to be a good leader. The essence of leadership is that in order to lead others, you must be able to lead yourself. To lead yourself, you need to know yourself, and, as a manager, you also need to get to know other people.

The ideal environment for an intrapreneur – the advert

I have learned both from my own personal experience and the interviews just how significant the views and approach of management are in terms of the intrapreneur's ability to bring about change and development. Ultimately, it is management that determines whether or not innovation will happen. That is not to suggest that management of intrapreneurs in a workplace is a simple matter, as it places specific demands both on leadership and on the work climate, as I have outlined previously. It is, of course, not easy to fulfil these requirements and conditions if a manager or colleague is unable to identify with them or take on board the implications.

I tried to think of the most helpful way to progress from a discussion of the theory to how things work in practice so that we have a clear picture of what it is we are talking about. In the end, I decided the solution was to **describe what was required to facilitate an intrapreneur's work in the form of** a tailored recruitment advert, written from the point of view of the intrapreneur. So the fictitious advert below presents a post that, as I see it, amply meets the requirements for successful intrapreneurship. Taken as a whole, it may look like nothing but a collection of fine words, but anyone who reads the text carefully will soon become aware of the complexities. Thus a stimulating challenge for a manager might be to consider the implications of the depiction of reality given in the advert and whether they are able to subscribe to it.

Advert
Wanted: a radical intrapreneur

"We're looking for someone who sees every challenge and problem as an opportunity and who loves what they do. You are someone who needs to understand how things work. You want opportunities to develop and to be a part of making our business even better. We would be delighted if you could help us find completely new solutions to existing problems and test out things we haven't tried before. You have an ability to see things from a variety of perspectives, and you understand, and can put into words, how the past, present and potential future fit together.

You are driven and guided in your work by your dreams and convictions about the future, and you are assured and fearless. You believe that you, and others, are capable of most things and that anything is possible, given the right conditions. You see opportunities where others see threats. This means that you are open, think big, and think differently, and are able to use your knowledge and imagination to identify possible new solutions to problems. Working in an atmosphere of uncertainty is seen as a challenge.

You have an excellent understanding of the organisation and an ability to assess other people's expertise and contributions. You base your work on your own ideas and visions about future potential, and you link these to the organisational vision. You drive processes forward with your patience and will-power, and you deal robustly with setbacks.

Selling is a strong point, and you have a persuasive and inspiring personality that makes it easy for you to form relationships. You are convinced that it is only possible to get results by working with other people. You are active, outgoing, curious and creative. You can put into words what is going on around you and inspire others to follow you. With your energy and enthusiasm, you make things happen; you have a strong belief in your own ability and that of others, and you are prepared to put in the effort in order to get results.

As your employer, we will give you a lot of freedom to organise your work and make your own decisions. We will provide financial resources and ensure you have the time you need. We will trust in your ability to get the right co-workers involved, focusing on your visions and goals as well as those of the organisation, and will be confident that you will make the most of the extensive cross-cutting skills of your colleagues and co-workers.

We realise that the chaos that you and your team will sometimes find yourselves in is in reality an essential and in some way structured creative process, and we will not attempt to control what you are doing. We understand and accept that you personally will not compromise on achieving your vision and that you may clash with people around you if they try to make you compromise on quality or interim goals. We realise that your strong drive to achieve results may conflict with the priorities and wishes of others.

Top management therefore undertakes to deal with any doubts or uncertainty that may arise elsewhere in the organisation while you are working on your project using unconventional methods and constantly questioning existing rules and structures. We will provide any necessary training and resources and eliminate skills gaps to enable your project to be as successful as it can be. We will make it clear that we have confidence in you and we will recognise and reward you and your team for your successes. And we accept the setbacks you will suffer, because we know that without setbacks there will be no successes to celebrate."

This rather too detailed advert includes most of the characteristics of an intrapreneur I have outlined previously. The advert also provides a general illustration of the type of employer and environment an intrapreneur needs to be able to innovate. This might be off-putting for managers who are used to tried and tested hierarchical structures and who find security in their planning processes, rules and strict frameworks. Not all owners and business leaders have the courage or desire to risk the long-term investment required to bring about radical innovation. Many companies cannot see beyond the next quarter and are judged only on their short-term results. Nor are all CEOs and senior managers prepared, or able, to let go of their traditional ways of working, including the control and the prestige that come with their roles, or, for that matter, to make changes to existing structures, rules and regulations.

And if top management does not have the courage to drive the process, we cannot expect middle management to do so. There needs to be open discussion within the organisation, at least at the top, about the type of innovation the organisation wants to engage in. Because, quite simply, if senior management is not motivated, or does not consider itself adequately equipped, to make the changes that an organisation aiming for continuous innovation needs in practice, there can be no innovation.

There is of course nothing wrong with owners and managers acquiring a detailed understanding of the implications of intrapreneurship and subsequently deciding against a strategy of radical innovation. But those whose rhetoric and visions are all about major investment in innovation but whose actions demonstrate the opposite – for example being risk averse, insisting on cost savings and stalling – will quickly lose the confidence of people across the organisation, in particular intrapreneurs and their team members. However creative the co-workers are, they will not step forward to drive innovation if the organisational climate is negative or neutral. They will only do so if the environment in the organisation is one that actively supports the creativity of the workers and innovation in general.

In addition, organisations need to adopt a strategic and long-term approach to their work, as there are examples of companies and organisations that have enjoyed short or longer successful periods of innovation but have gradually lost their ability to think afresh. Organisations that are unable to maintain a creative climate but instead begin to seek control by introducing new rules and procedures succeed only in stifling the organisation's innovative energy.

Are there actually any companies or organisations in existence that satisfy all the conditions in the advert? Any organisations featuring the optimum conditions for innovation, where the work climate and management are such that intrapreneurs are supported all the way? Read on for an interview with an intrapreneur who says that he does in fact work in the type of workplace described in the advert above.

Interview with N

I was curious for a long time about how things work in a workplace where intrapreneurship is a natural aspect of day-to-day activity. I began to wonder if such workplaces actually existed, as I had never once encountered one, either as an employee or as a consultant. But that was before I met N and heard his story.

Before the interview, other people described him as someone who was very successful at what he did, relationship-oriented and well-liked by a lot of people. A key person at his place of employment, he has undertaken many extremely important projects over the years.

"The main reason I am still here is because the work and the environment suit my personality. Everyone here is allowed to work entirely autonomously; we have complete freedom with responsibility. Even colleagues working in the kitchen or admin department make their own decisions, and the people working in the kitchen and restaurant are great at thinking up new ideas all the time ..."

N continues by describing how a co-worker or colleague who comes up with an idea is given every opportunity to put it into practice. "You're allowed just to get on with it. But you have to be prepared to take responsibility for the process and to manage it all yourself – everything from putting forward the initial idea to providing it with content and putting the whole thing into practice. It's the same for everyone. So yes, you could call me an intrapreneur, but then all my colleagues at work are intrapreneurs too."

N proves to be very pleasant and outgoing and quite a dominating person. He talks a lot – intensively and loudly – gesticulates vigorously and is the focus of attention, but is always extremely positive and engaging. He talks about his background and how, after college, he came into contact with an organisation that worked on coordination issues at both the local and national level. It was led by politicians and other stakeholders from the place where it was based. N describes how he fell into the organisation by accident when he was given the task of building up a regional training operation. A series of courses, lectures and drama workshops led to various types of conference on the subject, and, twenty years on, N is still with the same employer.

Asked whether he thinks there are any risks or immediate downsides to working with such a degree of autonomy and having freedom with responsibility, he says that almost everything is positive. "There's the odd occasion when I don't have support from my manager and people around me. Everyone is so busy working on their own projects. There can sometimes be drawbacks to being too productive, such as the time when I was a bit too heavily involved and my creativity took over – I had a constant flow of ideas and had to run several big projects at the same time. But it's usually possible to get a good balance between the various activities."

N tells how he came to have a role in the organisation's development work even at an early stage. Because it is largely a not-for-profit organisation, the only source of funding is money granted by politicians or funds generated by the employees themselves. When there was a financial crisis many years ago, N took it upon himself to develop a comprehensive programme of contract training which was offered out to various stakeholders. This brought a significant and necessary boost to the coffers. When I asked him directly, he confirmed that this has not been an isolated incident – on several occasions, he and his colleagues have found creative ways to bring money in to the organisation. He sees this as quite natural and not particularly remarkable.

What stimulates him most in his work otherwise is the opportunities he gets to meet a lot of interesting people. "I meet so many different, stimulating and interesting people when I'm working on my projects. It can be anyone from academic researchers and political decision-makers to artists and other stakeholders. It suits my personality very well, because it plays to my natural desire to learn and allows me to be associative and in a state of constant creative flow."

N confirms what others have said about him, that he is someone who is committed, talkative and very eager to learn, and is the focus of attention. He is also, as he himself admits, sometimes a little too bold. So, in view of his own personality, I wonder what sort of relationship he has with his manager. Does the fact that he is constantly coming up with ideas cause problems?

N says that there are no problems. He has great faith in his manager, who, in turn, shows that he trusts him and has confidence in him. His manager's general response is, "You can do this", and he is an inspiring person to bounce ideas off.

"My manager is a great source of inspiration for the whole organisation. If there's one negative in the way the organisation is managed, it would be that there's sometimes no structure linking the various co-workers and the projects. This is partly because everyone is driving their own project and partly because my manager prefers to have individual, visionary conversations with each person individually rather than with the group as a whole. That might be partly why it is becoming more difficult for the various intrapreneurs in the organisation to coordinate their work and collaborate."

I ask if he has discussed the issue of more coordination between co-workers with his manager. N says that he has, but that it is part of his manager's leadership style to have pep talks with each of them individually. This is not easy to change, as it seems to work both for the manager and for most of his colleagues. Now, N says, the effects of this are often more noticeable as the situation has changed in recent years. More employees have been taken on and so there are more people competing for the manager's attention.

"If you have an idea, there will still be a place for it, but there are now more people competing for resources – more of us are doing similar things. Also, there are now more and more strong individualists seeking to achieve personal fulfilment and whose guiding principle is 'it's my idea that matters' ..."

N says that he sees things differently from many of his colleagues. As a person, he is interested in science, in intellectual discussions about culture and in having the opportunity to "put what's happening into words". He is motivated by wanting to know more about things, while some of his younger colleagues, he feels, are more likely to ask, "What do the customers want?" to justify creating new projects on the basis of their own personal tastes.

I ask whether he finds that these generational differences affect the extent to which he and others are able to take on challenges and come up with innovative ideas and solutions to problems. N says that the major difference between then and now is that there used to be "big conversations about society". Previously, there might have been a discussion between a number of academics about what society stood for, whereas today there is more of an emphasis on individualism. The big danger now is that they end up focusing on superficial issues. However, he also points out that it is not surprising that there is a younger view of society and that part of the organisation's role is to make room for that and create space for diversity. This is the case even if there is quite a gap between the academics and those of his colleagues that he calls "the music coordinators".

While stressing that diversity is enriching and draws in resources, he points out that people also need to create time to listen to each other. A constant problem for his manager is deciding which projects to push forward and which to slow down. It can also be difficult to intercept problem employees when they are working with both freedom and responsibility. However, it is the manager's responsibility to define what is relevant to the task. So in a way, in N's view, this style of leadership can lead to competition between co-workers, and that might not be so positive.

Asked whether he feels restricted by the current situation, he says that, as the producer of events and exhibitions, he is able to continue asking questions to satisfy his curiosity. Although he has been working for twenty years, he has rarely been in a position where his ideas or projects have been obstructed. This is despite occasional jealousy on the part of colleagues who do not understand why his ideas are considered better than those of others.

At one point he found himself left out of the organisation's steering group, and realised that people around him were questioning his role. It was explained to him that this was because he was not a manager. After a while he was asked to return, as the other group members missed his creativity. They said that he was better than the rest of them at making clever connections between different ideas. He was a thinker attuned to the outside world, with a helicopter view, but also someone who thought in a different way to other people. He has now returned to the steering group.

What is it that drives him to continue to develop and to find challenges in the tasks he is working on? And what does he get out of identifying solutions and carrying out projects? N stresses that his main motivating factor is to do something better than it was done last time, and the challenge for him is in trying to do things in a different way. He is driven by his desire to learn and by social relationships. What he does must be challenging, creative and pleasurable; if it is not, he will choose to do something else. N sees himself as someone who asks questions and taps into the mood in the room, someone who is verbal, who thinks and talks at the same time, and who formulates his thoughts out loud. He puts things into words. He is also analytical, inspired and committed, and someone who opposes hierarchies and a silo mentality.

I finish by asking him what he thought made a successful project. His answer is indicative of the considerable demands he makes on himself in terms of shaping and carrying out the various projects. "You have to involve people, establish a positive dialogue and have trust and confidence in one another. The task must be generally meaningful for other people, at the same time as it is important to bring others with you and to be able to coordinate people and resources." N emphasises that the same fundamental requirements hold true for all projects. "They must be intellectually and/or practically challenging but you also need to have fun as you go."

A positive work climate and a manager who supports the intrapreneur

N is a good example of an intrapreneur employed in a workplace very similar to the one in the pretend advert above. He describes how he is happy with his work tasks, which he largely invents himself, and how he takes responsibility for formulating ideas and managing the creative processes while at the same time undertaking much of the implementation himself. N is very knowledgeable about his sector and shares the values and goals of the organisation. He sees himself as someone who is analytical, inspired and committed. He is driven by his intrinsic motivation, in the form of a sense of curiosity and a desire to learn, while also wanting to do things better than they were done before and to work with other people to create new things.

He thinks it is challenging to do things he has not done before that also enable him to develop. He is allowed to work autonomously with freedom and responsibility and is able to devote time to satisfying his curiosity and thinking in new ways, all things that are important for intrapreneurs. He is also able to influence both his own tasks and the overall picture, and is explicitly opposed to "hierarchies and a silo mentality". At the same time, he is prepared to take some risks to get results, and admits that he can be a little too bold, an indication that he feels secure at his place of work and undaunted by his challenges.

Typically, N does not initially identify as an intrapreneur, but he does agree that he is someone who goes a bit further than his colleagues in terms of identifying opportunities. He also admits that he has a specific ability to think differently, taking a helicopter view, something the steering group felt the loss of during the period when he was not part of it.

As an intrapreneur, he ensures that he is constantly meeting talented new people, and he collaborates both externally and internally with interesting colleagues. He insists on building relationships even if the organisation's resources are somewhat limited because of all the projects he and his colleagues are involved in. N appreciates the contact he has with other people and is good at selling his ideas. He feels that he is allowed to be committed, talkative and a focus of attention in the workplace, even if there is a certain amount of competition and jealousy.

Dialogue with his manager is seen as positive, encouraging and supportive. N is allowed to carry out most projects in the way he wants. However, his strong drive to achieve results may compete with his colleagues' own priorities and wishes. That means his manager has their hands full holding visionary conversations with each individual co-worker and establishing internal priorities between the different projects. It is a challenge for the manager to coordinate the work and resources to everyone's satisfaction, although it does appear to work really well.

It is clear from the above that it is possible to create a workplace that enables intrapreneurs to work to the best of their abilities. Even though the situation is different in every workplace and each one has its particular challenges, I am convinced that it is possible to create better conditions for innovation. But it is not enough for management to be aware of the importance of intrinsic motivation, a creative work climate and successful, credible leadership to drive different types of innovation. My starting point for Section 3 is about other factors that influence the intrapreneur and the work environment.

Is this knowledge sufficient to make us realise what we need to do to achieve innovation and how we need to do it? Or should there be further steps in our thinking process, and do we need to seek a more in-depth understanding of how we as people, with our different approaches, attitudes and behaviours, influence ourselves and others? Is this something that can, in turn, affect the extent to which the work climate paves the way to intrapreneurship and innovation? In the next section, I present research and ideas on the subject of positive attitudes, the importance of the brain for the ability to innovate and how we are influenced by conscious and unconscious attitudes. The section concludes by discussing the difficulties of communicating effectively and positively with people who are very different from ourselves and what we can do about it.

CHAPTER 3

FACTORS INFLUENCING THE INTRAPRENEUR AND THE WORK ENVIRONMENT

If an organisation is to achieve sustained success, the most important factor is its employees. Whatever their role, co-workers will have an effect on the organisation as a result of their personality, abilities and social skills.

Of course, some people are more important for the overall picture. Some have more of an impact on their surroundings than others because of their personality, while other people have a high degree of formal power and influence due to their positions.

In order to place the intrapreneur in a context, it is important to look at the whole picture. Both management and individual co-workers need to become more aware of how they as individuals can help shape their shared work environment. In this section, I aim to show how various factors contribute to, and possibly explain, the attitudes of both intrapreneurs and other co-workers and their ability to work together.

In doing this, I hope to be able to provoke some thinking around what lies behind various attitudes, and what, in turn, affects the ability of companies and organisations to innovate. I have done this by looking at many different factors and research findings and summarising each in a few pages. Topics include positivity, how our brains influence us and factors such as consciousness, will-power, patience and habitual behaviour.

Readers with specialist knowledge in any of these fields may find the text superficial, while others may feel that there are too many references to different pieces of research. Nonetheless, I am convinced that by looking at the whole picture we will achieve greater understanding. However complex reality is, there are ways of working on oneself and others to promote more successful attitudes, but the basis of it is self-awareness – a desire and a will to understand the effect I have on my environment and how I myself influence, and am influenced by, the people around me.

The importance of positive emotions for creativity and innovation

Research into positivity indicates that there are very strong connections between the success factors for intrapreneurship and a positive attitude. It is the theories on positivity that link the experiences of the interviewed intrapreneurs and the research in the previous section into factors affecting the ability to innovate. Both creativity and intrinsic motivation arise out of a positive attitude, which is in turn the basis of a creative work climate and successful, credible leadership.

Positive psychology as a branch of psychology has existed since 1998. The concept of positive psychology was introduced by the American psychologist Martin Seligman, who was president of the *American Psychological Association*. His message was that the science of psychology had spent too little time researching what was healthy in people and looking at what makes life worth living. Instead, researchers had been focusing for a long time on mental ill health. In positive psychology, researchers chose to look at healthy human conditions such as well-being, happiness and joy based on empirical data and studies.

The status of positive psychology as a science is not undisputed. It is questioned by representatives of other areas of psychology and some other researchers, with critics claiming that it lacks a sound scientific basis. In addition, research findings are sometimes used in a destructive way. People can become fixated about ideas such as "positive thinking" and "joy"; those in crisis are urged to deny the negative aspects of their lives and to "think adversity and sorrows away" through positive thinking. That way of thinking runs counter to the focus of research in positive psychology, as it is descriptive rather than normative. This does not mean that researchers recommend that people think positive thoughts; research simply looks at what happens with people who think positively.

Setting aside the critical voices, there are nonetheless many interesting aspects to positive psychology that have a bearing on both intrapreneurship and creativity. Of particular interest to me is Barbara Fredrickson's research. She has been studying social psychology, affective science and positive psychology for over twenty years, and is currently looking at how people's attitudes affect their mental and physical health.

Research by Fredrickson and her colleagues (2010) in the area of *"positive emotions and human flourishing"* has received widespread international recognition. The findings show that, by developing a positive attitude, we improve our ability to deal with problems, thus paving the way to both success and good health. Positive emotional experiences help us to broaden our minds and to be open to what is happening around us, making us more creative and more optimistic.

According to the research, positive people relate to others in a genuinely friendly way, which in turn means that people around them are generally happy to give them their support. Good relationships with other people give rise to new opportunities and help create more, and better, alternative solutions to problems and challenges. Positivity and openness thus reinforce one another. Researchers have been able to demonstrate that developing positivity can have both physical and psychological effects. Positivity means that we:

- Sleep better, have lower blood pressure, are at less risk of diabetes, get fewer colds and feel less pain. Good health increases our chances of living longer
- Become more open, making us more receptive and more creative
- Broaden our minds and become aware of new alternatives and options
- Become more resilient and more able to bounce back from adversity

The conclusion that positive emotions have a positive effect on health is based in part on research findings that show that negative emotions, such as stress, are harmful for the body. In stressful circumstances, the negative effects on the body include a higher pulse rate, higher blood sugar levels and a weakened immune system. If these physical reactions are not addressed after a period of stress, they may over time lead to ill health, including coronary artery disease, increasing the risk of premature death (Fredrickson 2000). There are studies that show how positive emotions can help those experiencing stress to relax and to find their way back to their basic physiological needs. According to Maslow's hierarchy, this includes avoiding pain, sleeping and keeping physically active.

Many different studies have looked at the extent to which positivity can increase creativity, openness and the ability to identify opportunities.

Methods have included testing visual attention and the ability to associate words by exposing test subjects to positive, negative and neutral stimuli. It has been found that when people feel positive, other abilities quickly develop. The broader the visual attention developed, the more verbally creative people become, while negative and neutral stimuli have no effect. Those experiencing more positive emotions are more able to cope with setbacks and stress than others. Their openness makes them even more accepting of other people, as they see similarities between themselves and others rather than differences.

Several factors are consistent with the intrapreneurial personality. The ability of a positive person to cope better with stress and adversity that is identified in the research is very much in line with the patience and resilience of an intrapreneur. In addition, intrapreneurs are open to differences and alternatives as part of their search for different kinds of solutions.

The Broaden-and-Build Theory

Fredrickson (2001) summarises the importance of positivity in human development in her "*broaden-and-build theory*". The theory suggests that positivity broadens by opening people's minds to more options, and builds by developing resources. This in turn brings us new opportunities and even more options. She concludes that the ability to be positive has been crucial to human development over millennia. Fredrickson sees the function of positive emotions as part of "natural selection" and as something that has increased an individual's chances of survival.

Over time, a positive attitude meant people developed increased personal abilities and better physical, social, intellectual and psychological resources. The ability to broaden and build meant people were more able to cope with future external threats. By working positively and willingly with others to create large groups and build communities, people acquired the security and resources they needed for their continued development. Fredrickson says that this was because positive emotions enhanced their ability to deal with problems.

A positive mindset generates more, and better, possible solutions to problems. Positive emotions and openness are mutually reinforcing, and it is easier to learn something new if we are open to new impulses or have a deep interest in a particular topic. Once we have learnt something, new horizons open up to us, giving us opportunities to learn even more. "Broadening and building" is something we do when we feel secure and our needs have been satisfied.

For Fredrickson, positivity is something that builds human resources over a longer period, whereas negativity has an immediate impact. Negative and neutral emotions narrow our range of vision. This is extremely useful when we need to react swiftly in a crisis, but it also restricts other abilities, such as the ability to build and develop. This is because the negativity means people have a tendency to withdraw and take refuge from other people and the world around us.

Fredrickson concludes from her research that a positive attitude is beneficial to the ability of the intrapreneur to be open to new opportunities and to seek creative solutions. That openness and positivity reinforce one another can be seen in intrapreneurs' descriptions of collaboration within the intrapreneurial team and in how the mutual reinforcement of positivity and openness generates an upward spiral.

About positive reinforcement

So, what is positivity exactly? According to Fredrickson (2010), patterns in the research findings suggest that a person's well-being is affected by small, but logical, individual differences in positive, emotional experiences. This is to do with the way in which individuals experience pleasant everyday events and whether they are able to find positive ways in which to reinforce them.

It is not just that people who flourish feel well and do good; people do good things *because* they feel well. Individuals with greater sensitivity to negative experiences are at risk of reinforcing negativity and becoming depressed, and, correspondingly, positive reinforcement can bring about and maintain well-being and creativity. So, a positive attitude comes about when we experience more positive emotions than negative emotions.

Fredrickson describes positivity as the fleeting feeling that arises in a situation when, for example, we feel close to another person, loved, playful, creative or in a silly mood. Because this positive feeling is subtle and transient, several separate, positive emotional experiences are needed before an effect can be felt. The positive emotions come out of how we think, i.e. how we interpret events, experiences, thoughts and ideas as they arise. We also need patience and to llow the emotions time to have an effect. To create positive emotions, we need to take time to identify things that are good and then allow the emotion associated with the thing that is good to grow stronger within us. Many people find it difficult to set aside the time needed to identify and experience what is positive. But it is important that we consciously decide to do this, because our brains, often without us being aware of it, are constantly being influenced by worry, demands, doubts and negative impulses from outside.

Fredrickson describes the overall effect of positive emotional experiences as

- Making us feel good
- Enabling us to train and change our frame of mind, e.g. influencing our will-power
- Creating resilience to negative influences
- Helping us achieve extraordinary results through enhanced creativity and openness

Emotions are linked to approach and attitude through a kind of cause-and-effect relationship. The research shows that positive experiences leave their mark and alter the brain, thus affecting how we relate to the world about us. In other words, it is possible to influence people's views of different options by making them feel good! Positivity, just like negativity, is contagious!

Fredrickson's research (2010) shows that there are different types of emotions – factors – that are crucial in terms of whether or not a person develops positivity and flourishes. These factors are associated with feelings of:

- Joy
- Gratitude
- Serenity
- Interest
- Hope
- Pride
- Amusement
- Inspiration
- Awe
- Love

For most of the ten positivity factors identified by Fredrickson, there is a direct connection with intrapreneurs and members of successful intrapreneurial teams. In my interviews, the intrapreneurs describe what it is that is characteristic of the collaboration in their teams. The positive work climate is demonstrated in the fact that team members are **interested** and **inspired** by their task. They feel **hopeful** that they will succeed in doing something really good and **believe** that the team will achieve its goals. They **trust** and **respect** each other, experience **joy** in their work and have **fun** together, at the same time as they are **inspired** and **convinced** that **anything is possible**. When they have achieved a goal, they feel a sense of **pride** and want to celebrate their success before they move on. Research into both intrapreneurship and successful teams provides proof that these factors really matter to a team's success.

About extraordinarily successful teams and the positivity ratio

Fredrickson's research, along with that of others, confirms that the positive attitude based on her ten factors really is important for achieving successful change. The best-known study is that of psychologist Macial Losada (2004), who investigated what it is that makes extraordinarily successful teams. He claims that there are clear mathematical relationships between the number of positive or negative emotions experienced by the people in a team and how successful they are.

Losada uses his own *Meta Learning Model* to examine sixty different corporate teams. The model describes the interpersonal dynamics of high, medium and low-performing teams based on an overall assessment of profitability and customer satisfaction and a 360-degree feedback survey. He shows that around 25 per cent of the teams were extraordinarily successful, while around 30 per cent achieved poor results and created dissatisfaction. The remaining 45 per cent had mixed results. Losada's study shows that what sets the members of the really successful teams apart is a very high level of positivity. Positivity is achieved by the team members acting creatively and supportively and talking to each other in an encouraging, helpful and approving way. To the outsider, Losada says, teams often seem chaotic and unpredictable, but if you look more closely you can see that there is a clear sense of order within what is a very complex structure.

Teams that have mixed results tend to stall because team members employ sarcasm, disapproval and cynicism, and they gradually lose their flexibility, joy and ability to ask questions. In comparison with the mixed groups, the high-performing teams have much greater resilience and are likely to achieve success more than once. The more negatively team members behave towards each other, the worse the team's performance. As they are part of a group, the attitudes of individuals rub off on other team members.

Like Fredrickson, Losada concludes that you need several positive emotions for every negative one for positivity to get the upper hand over negativity. When Fredrickson and Losada (2005) put forward their concept of the "positivity ratio", they attracted a good deal of attention from across the world. The positivity ratio is defined as the ratio of positive emotional experiences to negative ones.

Losada states that a high positivity ratio is very important for a team's success. He claims that mathematical calculations show that there is a specific breaking point at which both people and teams can achieve extraordinary results and also feel good in themselves. Working with Fredrickson, he suggested that a positivity ratio of 3:1 was "the tipping point" for individuals. He has also personally claimed that an extraordinarily successful team has a positivity ratio of 6:1.

A few years ago, when the research had been well-established and had been favourably regarded for almost ten years, the mathematical models in Losada's research came in for heavy criticism. Professor of physics Alan Sokal (2013) is one academic who completely rejects the idea of mathematically-relevant breaking points. He has demonstrated that the mathematical relationships on which Losada bases his conclusions do not actually exist.

That same year, Fredrickson decided to withdraw sections of the research findings published in 2005. Referring to the criticism of the mathematical modelling, she distanced herself from the statement that the breaking points were crucial in determining whether or not an individual would succeed and flourish. Fredrickson also (2013) insisted that those aspects of the study based on the findings from the psychological theory and quantitative data remain valid. She references the fact that, in recent years, several researchers have independently shown that the proportions of positive and negative emotional experiences *are* significant in terms of individual well-being. Where positive emotions and our health and happiness are concerned, it is a case of the more the better.

Fredrickson's later studies identify two limitations to the positive effect of positivity. She says that there is an upper limit to the benefits of positivity, at least in terms of positive emotions focused on the self. At very high levels of positivity, people may become complacent and indifferent, which has a negative effect on creativity. Excessive doses of self-focused positive emotions can also be damaging to people suffering from bipolar disorder.

Fredrickson's research data from the same studies show that, where negative emotions are concerned, the fewer the better. However, that only applies down to a certain level. She says that the negativity either supports healthy functions or destroys them, depending on the context and the size of the dose of negativity in relation to the positive emotions. A very low dose of negativity combined with a high dose of positivity has been shown to be beneficial for creativity.

Researchers of repute such as Jim Kouzes and Barry Posner (2010) refer to Fredrickson's research in their book, where they assert the significance of positivity. They demonstrate, through their own research, that positive reinforcement is important and that exemplary leaders are both positive and optimistic. Fredrickson's research on the influence of positivity tallies with the discoveries of other researchers. For example, the idea that positivity broadens minds and enhances creativity is very much in line with Teresa Amabile's (2011) research on creativity. Losada's observations that the members of successful teams support each other in a creative and positive way and talk positively to one another matches both my own experiences and those of other intrapreneurs.

Furthermore, Losada's contention that "to the outsider, teams often seem chaotic and unpredictable, but yet there is a clear sense of order within what is a very complex structure" is consistent with the research and the intrapreneurs I have interviewed.

The research into positivity sets out the ways in which companies and organisations can create the corporate culture that intrapreneurship needs. Some people may feel that discussing positivity at all is a woolly-headed diversion, but, as shown in the previous section, researchers do believe that a positive attitude is significant and take the idea seriously. This is true whether we are talking about the necessary conditions for creativity, for intrinsic motivation or for leadership, all of which are important factors in successful innovation.

To avoid any misunderstanding, I must emphasise that positivity is not a quality or behaviour that can be forced on anyone, nor should it be used as some sort of doctrine to be strictly adhered to by all. It would be a dreadful state of affairs if a co-worker were punished or openly picked on for expressing a valid criticism or failing to immediately acclaim every change proposed by management. I have seen instances where managers, usually without the knowledge of their seniors, have used positivity as an instrument of power. If a manager demands a consistently positive attitude of his co-workers, many of them will be afraid to challenge anything. As a result, the mutual trust and confidence between managers and co-workers will decline or be lost completely, making successful innovation very difficult.

Positivity is a basic prerequisite for the ability to innovate, alongside a number of other factors. There follows a review of what researchers have to say on how our brain influences our thoughts, emotion and behaviours, followed by a closer look at the power of habit, will-power and the role of patience.

The importance of the brain for the ability to innovate

The fact that the brain is crucial to our functioning comes as no surprise. Psychologists have been studying human behaviour for a long time, and in recent years there have been groundbreaking developments in neuroscience, the study of the brain. The boundaries between the various professions are being erased as researchers ask questions about the intricate workings of the brain and what it influences and is influenced by. This includes research into how processes in the brain and nervous system affect our thoughts, feelings and behaviours.

There have been theories on how thoughts and feelings interact for hundreds of years, and laboratory experiments have been carried out on both humans and animals. In some periods we have believed that thoughts govern feelings, while at other times we have thought the opposite. What is new is that technological developments are increasingly enabling us to monitor the neurological reactions when the human brain is subjected to different kinds of stimuli. Although new technology has increased our knowledge, it has also made researchers aware of how little we actually know about how different parts of the brain interact and what influences our thoughts, feelings and behaviours.

This has meant that it has become more common for knowledge from different fields to be combined. Professor Lisa Feldman Barrett (2009) is one acknowledged pioneer of interdisciplinary research into emotional states, combining affective neuroscience with psychological studies of the construction of personality and emotion. She believes that thoughts and feelings are concepts that have no basis in the brain, and says in an interview that "emotion and cognition are considered processes in the mind and brain, and need to be explained. But there is growing evidence that the brain does not respect this division." Her research questions the widespread perception that feelings are universal and recognisable and that they exist in different places in the brain. Instead, she believes, feelings are created in the moment, through interplay between all the brain's basic systems, and they can be influenced by lifelong learning.

However, other researchers cling to the notion of thoughts and feelings as separate concepts, not least because the words fit well with the mental processes being studied. This separation of thoughts and feelings is the basis on which I describe below some of the brain's different areas and functions. The aim is to give readers an overview and general understanding of various neurological relationships. The section includes examples of interesting results from current research into the brain.

I have focused on showing different researchers' views of the importance of the brain for qualities and behaviours that are, or may be, important for the ability to innovate. This includes concepts such as willpower, patience and the ability to make decisions, which are some of the qualities characteristic of the intrapreneur. It also covers attitudes to risk-taking, and how we create and are controlled by our habitual thoughts.

Different parts of the brain and how they affect us

Driving innovation is the same as driving constant change. Change is not something our brains are programmed simply to accept.

Learning more about how the brain works makes it easier to understand why we act and react as we do in different situations. Attempting to gain an understanding of when and how we use our brain to make active decisions is an interesting process. What makes us react instinctively and/or stick to a habit, whether it is good for us or not?

The human brain is complex and unique with a range of different functions, and there is constant activity in all its different parts. Several important areas of the brain affect human behaviour and our ability to create different types of habits. They have different core functions but they communicate continuously with each other and the rest of the body through the signalling of nerve cells. The areas I introduce here are the prefrontal cortex, basal ganglia, limbic system and reptilian brain[1].

Thinking, processing and making decisions

Unique to human beings is the prefrontal cortex (PFC), the front part of the cortex. The PFC is the seat of abilities such as refraining from responding to stimuli and planning movements and actions. It controls our ability to think abstractly and logically, our linguistic ability, and our ability to remember and to create context. These are activities that enable us to think, process information and make decisions. The PFC performs sophisticated actions that have overall control of our behaviour and is in constant communication with other parts of the brain. Various activities are begun and controlled here, but the PFC also controls and checks undesirable behaviour. Empathy, and the ability to adapt to social contexts, belong to this part of the brain, and it is likely that the feeling of motivation begins with activity in these groups of nerve cells. The PFC is highly active when we are learning new, complex behaviours, but activity in this area declines as a thing becomes routine and subsequently a habit.

Professor Robert Sapolsky (2004) claims that as the human brain developed and grew, the PFC too became bigger and acquired new functions. Now, Sapolsky says, the PFC controls what you choose to pay attention to, what you think about and even how you feel. He believes that its chief function is to influence people, to make them do "the harder thing".

For example, when it is easier for you to:

- Stay on the sofa – your prefrontal cortex makes you want to get up and take some exercise
- Say yes to dessert – your prefrontal cortex remembers the reason why you ought to order tea instead
- Put a project off until tomorrow – your prefrontal cortex will help you switch on your computer and start work

The brain influences us more than we think

We make numerous decisions every day, and the most common of these involve choosing whether to do something or refrain from doing it. This does not mean that our decisions are always conscious or more complex decisions made after careful consideration, such as those we make with the help of the prefrontal cortex. Our quick "yes/no" decisions are the result of chemical processes in an area called the striatum, part of the basal ganglia. The basal ganglia are found in both halves of the brain and play an important role in decision-making, learning and various motor functions.

We might ask whether it is normal not to want to change. Do you get frustrated when you ask someone if they want to do something special, or something new and different, and they answer "No" almost without thinking? Or are you yourself the sort of person who hesitates when faced with something new, and spontaneously reacts negatively to "challenging" suggestions from other people? If so, you are not alone.

In 2015, researchers Jyotika Bahuguna, Ad Aertsen and Arvind Kumar published a new computational model, which shows that the "Go" and "No-Go" signals that originate in the nerve cells in the striatum compete in the brain. The study presents an exciting, theoretically-possible explanation showing how human beings may be wired to be "natural naysayers".

The striatum, the largest of the structures in the basal ganglia, contains two different groups of nerve cells – D1R neurons and D2R neurons. Researchers call these "Go" and "No-Go" respectively, and they are controlled by the neuromodulator dopamine. The Go neurons and the No-Go neurons follow their own separate pathways in the brain and are linked in such a way that they both compete with and inhibit each other. When we are faced with alternatives and have to make a choice, the striatum acts as a decision threshold for signals from other parts of the brain, such as the cortex. Researchers say that the No-Go neurons inhibit Go neurons more strongly than the other way around, because the No-Go pathway is stronger from the outset. They therefore conclude that the standard response programmed into our brains is "No".

However, researchers have shown that, even if the spontaneous response is "No", there are various ways of influencing the likelihood of the Go signal being stronger than the No-Go. In order to facilitate a positive decision, the individual needs to be stimulated, and this can be done in various ways. One way is to adjust the threshold with the help of the neuromodulator dopamine, perhaps through other people influencing an individual to make a positive decision. This could be by means of skillful marketing, peer pressure or persuasion. Another way is through increased learning and knowledge that makes it possible for the individual to learn more about themselves and train themselves to make conscious decisions.

It is interesting that the researchers claim that we are all able to influence our spontaneous "No" reflex. This can be done either through voluntary or involuntary exposure to strong external influences, which is a variation of external motivation, or by an individual strengthening their internal motivation. The latter involves learning more about their motivations and how they themselves function so as to strengthen the Go signal. Those who are aware of how this works can thus avoid falling into restrictive thought patterns.

Ann Graybiel (2013), who has studied the importance of the striatum for patterns of thought, learning and habits, has demonstrated, amongst other things, that habits create patterns in the brain. Her research shows that the cortex and striatum cooperate to create habits by clustering together to form what are known as matrisomes. Graybiel has also demonstrated how patterns of neural activity are created when a habit is formed. The nerve cells are activated when we initialise a habit, but they are only active at the beginning and end of the habitual activity and are quite passive in between. This is why it costs us less energy to do something habitual than to make active decisions.

Emotional reward

Neuroscientists often talk about the human reward system. This consists of the networks in the central nervous system that regulate and control our behaviour by influencing our feelings of enjoyment. Human behaviour is based on stimulating things that provide feelings of happiness and wellbeing and avoiding things that are unpleasant by reacting appropriately when danger threatens.

A psychological reward is a process that reinforces a behaviour at the biochemical level by means of neuromodulators, in particular dopamine. The process affects the limbic system, also known as the "emotional brain", which is located deep in the cerebrum. This is a series of different brain structures that researchers have up to now thought responsible for human survival, for example in the form of emotions during stress reactions and flight responses, feelings of love and desire for sex. It is the seat of the more intuitive processing that is associated with judgemental functions and emotions/feelings, and it plays an extremely important role in memory and learning. In very simplified terms, it is when dopamine floods out from nerve fibres in the brain's reward system and stimulates specific receptor molecules on other nerve cells that we experience pleasure!

The limbic system includes an old and primitive structure called the amygdala. This comprises the groups of nerve cells that manage memories linked to emotional situations. Neuroscientists Katarina Gospic, Professor Martin Ingvar (2011) and others have shown in a study that humans appear to have an inbuilt ability to respond to injustices, and that this response stems from the amygdala. The amygdala is responsible for our rapid decisions – it judges if something is dangerous or safe, good or bad, and then responds. The decision is not based on any detailed information, it is a black or white response. These emotional reactions have a major role to play in assessing risk and are also important for our feelings of motivation.

The level of activity in the amygdala varies from individual to individual, and research shows that low activity can result in some people being more inclined to take risks than others. They choose to take greater risks despite being aware at the intellectual level that there may be a danger involved. Conversely, people with an active amygdala that flags up danger and creates unpleasant emotions tend to avoid high-risk situations. In order to avoid these unpleasant feelings and reactions, such people become risk averse. The emotional responses take place milliseconds before the individual is aware of what is happening and therefore influence the choices they make.

There are other areas where reactions in the amygdala play a significant role. Gospic's research shows that the amygdala actively manages feelings of injustice. The greater the activity in the amygdala, the more the individual processes injustices they have experienced, and they may even refrain from certain activities because they are in themselves unfair.

A study by Feldman Barrett shows that the amygdala can contribute to more negative emotional interpretations of situations through increased sensitivity to negative stimuli. Experiments have shown that, when looking at negatively-charged images, there is a stronger response in the amygdala in those people who have experienced a lot of stress and fear than in those who have not experienced negative emotions previously.

It is interesting to consider the importance of the activity of the amygdala for the ability to innovate. A low level of activity in the amygdala increases the tendency to take risks while a high level increases the sense of perceived injustice, which suggests that the level of activity in the amygdala for intrapreneurs may be relatively low. Of even more interest is the strong response to stress and fear. The more fearful and uncertain a person is, the less inclined they probably are to change, whether in their private life or in the workplace. A person who feels safe and secure, meanwhile, will be more prepared to contribute to change. These conclusions tally with Fredrickson's "broaden-and-build theory", which suggests that the ability to be positive has been crucial to human development throughout the ages.

Fundamental needs

Finally, there are certain functions linked to human survival that are regulated by the part of the brain that we refer to informally as "the reptilian brain." It includes parts of the brain stem, the cerebellum and the oldest part of the cerebrum in evolutionary terms. The reptilian brain controls involuntary functions such as breathing, blood pressure, pulse, balance, wakefulness and sleep. The brain stem is the main communication route between the brain, the spinal cord and the peripheral nervous system. Some scientists like to include the amygdala in this group.

The reptilian brain works as a reflex and is linked to abilities such as finding food, the fight or flight response in the face of danger, and reproduction. Put very simply, the reptilian brain takes over when the cerebrum is not working properly. This might be in the event of acute physical or mental stress, such as starvation, intense fear or when someone has consumed too much alcohol.

From the point of view of innovation, in other words, aspects of our defence mechanisms against change can be explained as the interplay of neurological signals in the brain. That might be an automatic No-Go in the striatum or a negative response from the amygdala to something perceived as dangerous and stressful.

However much we may want to believe that we make rational decisions by thinking, science demonstrates that there are no simple truths. Feldman Barrett and her colleagues have shown that the cortex is active in an enormous number of processes that have been classified as emotional. At the same time, the amygdala and other deep-lying nuclei are involved in what we call thinking. Not only that, the interplay between the prefrontal cortex and the amygdala is also very important in terms of our habits and the extent to which we can influence them using willpower and patience. These are the same abilities intrapreneurs use when driving their projects. The next section is about research into how these qualities function and, by extension, how they might manifest themselves in intrapreneurs.

Willpower

What is willpower exactly, and how can we influence it?

When things do not turn out as we had imagined, it is easy to blame our lack of will, or a lack of will in the people around us. Many of us believe our lives would have been different if we had only had more of what we know as "willpower". We are convinced that with a bit more self-control, we could be more successful in achieving both our private goals and our goals at work. That might be personal goals, such as improving our health by eating healthier food, exercising regularly and avoiding sweets, drugs and alcohol, or other socially acceptable goals – we might aim to save money rather than throw it away or to stop procrastinating at work.

In the foreword to his book on the theory of relativity (1916), Einstein wrote that he realised readers would probably need "a fair amount of patience and force of will" to get through the book. Distinguishing between patience and willpower is not a straightforward task.

Dictionaries tell us that willpower is an internal drive to get one's own way, a drive based on patience and commitment. It is the same thing as self-control and the ability to determine one's own actions. We might also describe it as the ability to resist short-term satisfaction so as to achieve more long-term goals. The opposite to using one's willpower is allowing oneself to be governed by impulse and emotions.

Ever since the researcher Walter Mischel presented his famous "Marshmallow Experiment" (1972) forty years ago, researchers have been more or less in agreement over how we should view willpower from a psychological perspective. In the meantime, researchers have been active in the fields of both neuroscience and psychology, and the two areas have cross-fertilized each other. But recently new research has mounted a strong challenge even to well-established psychological truths. Whichever of the theories prove at a later date to be the most accurate, they are nonetheless relevant to the debate about people's ability to innovate.

Mischel's study was originally a study of willpower in children; he investigated whether young children could defer a reward – a marshmallow in this case – so as to get a greater reward later. His study shows that only 30 per cent of the children were able to wait. Researchers say that those children able to wait for a reward are using their prefrontal cortex, i.e. the part of the brain that is linked to thinking and cognitive reflection and does not particularly have a 'tempting' function. The children who defer are able to divert their attention from the reward while they are waiting by thinking about something else. Their behaviour is different from that of the other children, who instead use the limbic system to smell and imagine tastes. According to the study, the results are better when the children are given tips on how to "think coldly" so that they can resist temptation. They also improve if the children trust the person leading the experiment, as the children who have confidence in the leader are better at deferring the reward.

Mischel's later research shows that test subjects who demonstrate strong willpower as children usually have good self-control as adults too. The opposite is true for those whose willpower is poor when they are tested as children. When faced with challenges as adults, they continue to be more easily influenced by emotions and impulses. According to the research, when exposed to temptation, test subjects with poor willpower exhibit brain patterns that are different to those of people with strong willpower. They are more impulsive and less considered in their actions, find it more difficult to concentrate and to learn new things, and also find it harder to remember what they have learnt.

Willpower, in Mischel's view, is like a muscle that can be exercised but that also gets tired when over-used. Studies show that when people are repeatedly having to resist temptation or are constantly exposed to will-related pressures, their ability to resist temptation or endure difficult situations in the future declines. Researchers now agree that the exercising of self-control does cause mental fatigue, something that has been debated for over a hundred years. They do not, however, agree *why* this is the case.

The psychologist Roy Baumeister (1998) is an influential researcher in the field of willpower and self-control. The thrust of Baumeister's theory is that willpower is dependent on a physical energy, and that this energy can be temporarily sapped by various kinds of cognitive tasks and the exercising of willpower. He is referring to tasks that require us to control our reactions by overriding, preventing or changing an emotional state, a need, a thought or a behaviour. If the physical energy is temporarily reduced by a demanding task, there may be less mental strength, and therefore less self-control, to be applied to subsequent tasks.

A person who exerts too much self-control may experience mental exhaustion. Baumeister coined the term "ego depletion" to describe a situation in which a person has temporarily depleted their mental energies. He says that in the instance of, for example, extreme or lasting stress, significant demands on concentration or a lack of sleep, the ego is depleted, whereupon there is a decline in self-control. Diminished self-control impairs many conscious and will-driven processes, such as will-driven choice, the ability to take control of a situation, and being prepared for and initiating new challenges. It becomes difficult to withstand temptation or to refrain from acting on reasoned, but undesirable, responses to various stimuli.

Because the prefrontal cortex needs a lot of energy for it to function, the level of glucose in the blood is important in terms of the amount of energy the brain has access to. According to Mischel's research, people with poor willpower have considerably lower levels of blood glucose to begin with than those with strong willpower. In the early part of the 2000s, Baumeister and other researchers linked the limited mental energy that Baumeister called ego depletion with a lack of real energy in the form of glucose (Gailliot & Baumeister 2007). Several studies from that time show that mentally fatigued people have lower blood sugar levels than those with strong willpower. It is thought, therefore, that a lack of self-control is more likely when glucose levels are low or the glucose cannot be used effectively by the brain (i.e. when insulin levels are low or ineffective).

The researchers identify situations in which low glucose levels can lead to negative behaviour, such as problems with concentration and difficulties in being able to stop smoking and manage stress. There may also be problems that affect other people, for example an absence of guilt feelings and aggressive behaviour. In addition, there is research that shows that people lacking in mental energy (experiencing ego depletion) may have more stereotypical attitudes and be less willing to change the way they think (Glaser

& Knowles 2008). There is also evidence from research that ego depletion makes people less helpful and less forgiving to those around them.

Because the need is to gain control of internal impulses rather than conscious choices, there are methods we can use to improve our self-control. By predicting and planning for situations where we will probably have less willpower, we can prevent problems and avoid temptation. This might mean avoiding doing something important that requires concentration or not going shopping when we are tired and hungry after a day's work. But there are also ways in which we can boost our willpower.

Exercise your willpower and give your body energy

Several researchers, Baumeister included (2011), claim that we can improve our willpower by using it. Just like any other muscle, our willpower quickly tires after use but gets stronger over the long term. With consistent training, self-control practised on a regular basis can lead to stronger willpower. Mental training such as yoga or mindfulness, using the "wrong" hand or practising good posture can train our willpower and bring about a general improvement in our self-control.

The brain uses a good deal of energy, and studies show, as noted above, that willpower is affected by how much fuel – glucose, or blood sugar – the brain has access to. Some researchers believe that when we make an effort to maintain our self-control, the brain uses more glucose than it receives. They say that additional carbohydrates will improve willpower that has been weakened. Regular, healthy meals and proper sleep are also good for our willpower.

Other ways to improve willpower

We can mitigate the effects of weakened willpower by putting ourselves into a positive frame of mind with positive beliefs and attitudes, thus creating an environment that allows the "willpower muscle" to rest. It is important to avoid stressful environments that require major adjustment on the part of the individual, as they strain the "muscle" and make us less able to cope with new challenges. Diminished willpower in one area may also mean diminished willpower in other areas. This means it is more effective to focus on one goal at a time instead of doing too many demanding things at once.

We can also curb a decline in our willpower through our own ideas and attitudes. Researcher Mark Muraven (2012) and his colleagues claim that people controlled by social signals, and who feel they have to exercise self-control to please others, lose more of their willpower than those driven by their own internal goals and desires. Depletion of self-control can be affected by an individual's frame of mind, their attitude to the activity that requires self-control – the thing that "has to be done" – and their ability to replace the resources lost.

He says that depleted people are less positive about their abilities, have less sense of control and are less optimistic about the future. They make fewer demands on themselves and have less confidence in their ability to achieve a goal than non-depleted people. Muraven notes that optimistic perspectives and positive dreams are clearly not things that arise by themselves; an individual must be able to actively choose not to entertain doubt and negativity.

The process model – challenging the resource model

But research is continuously developing, and in recent years researchers have presented new findings and competing theories. According to the researchers Michel Inzlicht and Brandon J. Schmeichel (2012, 2013), the concept of self-control is easily understood without the need for discussions about "limited resources" and a lack of energy. They do not question the idea that willpower is depleted after a demanding task, but they do claim that there is no evidence to suggest that the depletion is caused by low levels of glucose or limited resources.

They call the alternative model that they have put forward "the process model of self-control depletion". This suggests that the depletion of willpower has the effect of changing an individual's intrinsic motivation. The mental fatigue causes the individual to shift their attention away from the taxing tasks that require control onto more gratifying tasks. Inzlicht and Schmeichel see self-control as an ability that has evolved to create a balance between multiple priorities – we care very much about our current happiness and enjoyment but are also keen to have stability and happiness in the future. It has always been a challenge to find a balance between immediate reward and the short-term discomfort or inconvenience needed to reap benefits in the future. Researchers see this as a balance in switching between the prioritisations for various tasks – switching between "have-to goals" and "want-to goals". "Have-to tasks" are those arising from a sense of duty or contractual obligation, whereas "want-to tasks" are done because they are enjoyable and meaningful at the time they are being carried out.

Inzlicht and Schmeichel say that people generally oppose tasks, such as work and other "must dos", that are taxing and do not provide any internal reward. There is no evolutionary benefit to using most of our time planning for the future, especially if it means we are not looking after ourselves in the present. We may still choose to engage in onerous, cognitively-controlled activity as and when we think it appropriate. However, it is something we find taxing, and it causes mental fatigue. This fatigue, or exhaustion, further alters our motivation, steering us away from labour-intensive, externally-motivated activities to the type of activity that provides intrinsic motivation and makes us feel good. Doing what we want to do restores the balance.

According to the researchers, whether or not something is perceived as fatiguing depends on whether the activity involves some sort of reward. Feeling entertained, being able to compete, experiencing fellow feeling with someone or having an interest in an activity make that activity rewarding, and the work does not then seem taxing. But doing something out of a sense of duty or contractual obligation, without any direct reward, *is* fatiguing.

It is the situation itself that determines whether or not something is taxing, and each of us has specific limits on the amount of effort we are prepared to put in before we need a break. There is no biological limit to self-control. The more exertion and fatigue we perceive, the greater the need for instantly enjoyable activities and the more our attention becomes focused on pleasant stimuli. Researchers claim that those people who can control their lives without having to deal with externally-imposed demands, have good habits and are engaged in difficult but rewarding activity do not experience mental fatigue.

Inzlicht and Schmeichel emphasise that the process model provides a starting point for an understanding of self-control and that more research is needed to investigate the effect on self-control of cognitive, motivational and affective factors. Inzlicht has worked with Zoe Francis (2016) to investigate the causes of ego depletion in greater depth.

It is obvious that willpower is an important factor in enabling an intrapreneur to drive innovation. Additionally, an intrapreneur needs a good deal of patience and resilience to be able to deal with processes, temporary setbacks and internal resistance to change.

Patience and resilience

Patience is an approach we take to external factors, i.e. circumstances that we have no control over ourselves. Having patience is having perseverance, an ability to wait without losing interest. It is allowing things to take their course and not expecting things to happen immediately. Patience is also endurance, the ability to keep one's cool while dealing with difficulties and setbacks, and being able to accept disappointment. A very patient person can cope with external stress without giving way to uncontrolled emotional outbursts, which is one reason why patience is often presented as a virtue.

Patience is one of the prerequisites for willpower; the other is commitment. The journalist Malcolm Gladwell is partly known for his book *Outliers: The Story of Success* (2008), in which he writes about the importance of patience in achieving success. He refers to research undertaken by the psychology professor Anders Ericsson, which shows that it takes ten thousand hours, the equivalent of about ten years' work, to become really successful in any particular field. He claims that the time invested is more important than any inborn talent. In recent years, the findings have been questioned by others including Ericsson himself, as his subsequent research has shown that many professionals have not needed ten thousand hours specifically because they do have an inborn talent or because other individual circumstances come into play.

Today, things move so fast that we may wonder what function patience actually has in either practical or psychological terms. Most long-term goals and innovations do require patience as we need to be able to keep doing things over and over again, sometimes making mistakes and sometimes getting it right, without succumbing to stress and frustration. The downside to having too much patience can be that we find it difficult to set limits and decide when to say stop. Having endless patience can also mean that matters are not brought to a head when they should be so that issues can continue to rumble on for too long, which is not good for either the individual, the project or the organisation.

The ability to be patient varies from person to person, and it has been shown that different cultural environments favour different amounts of patience. Patience is also affected by external circumstances and can vary over time. Research shows that there is connection between people's patience and their expectations in terms of speed. It is sometimes claimed that the rapid technological developments of our age mean that we increasingly have less patience. An example of this is a study by researchers S. Shunmuga Krishnan and Ramesh K. Sitaraman (2012) that shows how, when people view a video clip, the amount of patience they exhibit is affected by the internet speed they are used to. They note that those users who are used to a fast fibre-based internet connection abandon a video that is being slow to load up more quickly than users who are used to a slower internet connection, such as via a mobile. The users who were used to a better connection lost patience after only two seconds.

The question is whether we humans are approaching a time when our new generations have no need to improve their reserves of resilience and patience. If that is the case, what might that mean for our overall ability to innovate? Most long-term goals and innovations need patience as sometimes things will go wrong and we have to be able to deal with those situations as they arise.

As a group, intrapreneurs recognise themselves in descriptions that use words such as willpower, resilience and patience. They say that these are essential qualities because it takes time and energy to implement change. Strong intrinsic motivation, a belief in their own ability and that of their team and a long-term perspective all combine to develop an intrapreneur's resilience. It is an essential quality, since ideas and their implementation can often encounter significant opposition from both management and, especially, the rest of the organisation.

However, resilience is not always the same thing as patience; several intrapreneurs describe how they more or less force their plans through and, if this does not work, they resort to working in secret. Sometimes they are seen as really difficult people who are constantly making demands on others, irrespective of whether these are managers, colleagues or co-workers. For some, it seems that the challenge itself, including the struggle to make their own ideas a reality, is an important part of why they continue to be intrapreneurs.

The importance of the brain for the development of habits

Understanding more about how the brain works makes it easier to understand why we react as we do in different situations. When and how do we use our brain to make active decisions? What makes us react instinctively and stick to a habit, whether or not it is good for us? We can develop a habit by repeatedly behaving in a way that results in a pleasurable experience, a psychological reward, until eventually we do it without thinking.

Habits leave traces in the brain

As I mentioned previously, research shows that positive experiences leave their mark and alter the brain. Similarly, people's habits leave traces in the brain (Calakos & O'Hare, 2016; Graybiel, 2013; Olson, 2011).

The habits we develop either satisfy fundamental human needs that are essential for our survival or make us feel good or provide some other type of emotional reward. Habits make our lives easier as they reduce stress levels in the body. Sticking to a habit uses less energy than doing something new. Examples are cleaning our teeth twice a day, eating the same thing for breakfast, doing the same journey to work and going to the same place for lunch every day. Other examples of habits might be the way in which we view the people around us and how we address and respond to them.

Habits help us to organise our existence and meet a whole range of physical and psychological needs without us having to think about them. Bad habits, such as smoking, eating unhealthy food or drinking too much alcohol, are no different from good habits in this respect, as all habits fulfil a function. The brain does not differentiate between good and bad habits, and once we have created an "automatic" routine we will have formed a habit which can be difficult, but not impossible, to break.

Habitual thinking and thinking traps

We like to think of ourselves as rational decision-makers. In actual fact, between 80 and 90 per cent of our decisions are made using automatic decision-making processes in the brain. These processes provide a way for us to sift through all the information we receive so that we can make fairly accurate assessments with our limited mental capacity and make rational decisions when it is really necessary. Despite this, we humans generally have well-controlled, predictable and effective reactions and behaviours that actually work. We live with a lot of different parallel processes going on and are able to make them function. Proof of this is in the fact that most people manage to get up in the morning, go to work, perform their duties, maintain relationships and use their spare time largely as they want, in accordance with their personal goals. In other words, our automatic "habitual thinking" is very useful to us.

Several researchers representing different psychological orientations base their investigations of, and attempts to explain, different types of human attitudes and behaviours on the same theory – the *Dual Process Theory*. The central thesis is that we humans are equipped with two different types of cognitive systems, the first of which features an intuitive, unconscious and automatic process and the second an explicit, conscious, rule-based process. The first process is associated with our immediate, simplified reactions and the second with conscious, more considered decisions. Only humans have access to the latter system, which is seen as a consequence of evolution.

The more interconnected neuroscience and psychology become, the more obvious it becomes that the two systems cannot be identified. Because of this, they are currently used more as a theoretical construction with which to explain human behaviour. In a study in 2000, researchers Keith Stanovich and Richard West came up with the more neutral concepts of "System 1" and "System 2", putting forward suggestions as to how existing theories can be incorporated into each concept. According to their definition, both systems are continuously collaborating with each other. "System 1" works automatically, without effort, making quick-fire assessments based on familiar patterns, while "System 2" requires more mental effort and intense focusing.

The psychologist and Nobel laureate Daniel Kahneman (1979) undertook research in the field of behavioural economics with his colleague Amos Tversky, formulating what is known as *The Prospect Theory*. It describes how people respond to risk and shows how we make intuitive statistical decisions in which we judge anticipated gains and losses completely differently. According to the researchers, we have a tendency to overvalue both small probabilities and losses in relation to gains. The Prospect Theory contradicts established economic theories that describe how people make rational decisions by maximising benefits. Kahneman uses the System 1 and 2 concepts to explain what lies behind these irrational decisions.

In his book *Thinking, Fast and Slow* (2011), he provides more of a popular science explanation of what happens when people use their unconscious intuition, i.e. System 1, to make important decisions. He presents System 1 as a quick, lean, intuitive and indiscriminate process, while System 2 is more methodical, reflective and discriminating. Kahneman says that System 2 is relatively slow and is usually in standby mode until "called upon" by System 1.

System 1 is continuously in operation and enables us to do things such as drive a car and talk on a mobile phone at the same time without having to think about what we are doing. We can continue doing this until something unexpected happens that demands our attention, whereupon we have to call on System 2. It is because of System 2 that we stop automatically when we have to answer more complicated questions, because they require attention and focus. On the whole, the systems interact without difficulty, but Kahneman has identified situations where our use of System 1 leads to us making certain systematic mistakes. He provides examples of various thinking traps that System 1 may give rise to. By describing them, Kahneman aims to help us avoid or limit the damage that can be caused by incorrect judgements and irrational decisions.

One example of a thinking trap is when people prefer to construct a simple narrative about a complex reality. We attempt to identify the causes of random happenings, and believe that rare situations are probable. We also give greater weight to our own experiences. *"Confirmation bias"* is the term Kahneman uses to describe our tendency only to see, seek and interpret information that supports what we already think while disregarding anything that conflicts with it. Another term he uses is *"Base rate neglect"*, by which he means that we allow ourselves to be governed by our intuition when obliged to make complex judgements about probabilities. We draw conclusions by assigning greater importance to specific, new information than to original information that is general but relevant. *"Priming"*, on the other hand, is how we quickly and unconsciously link one concept to another, thus starting off a chain of associations in a specific direction.

The most important piece of advice he gives us is to think more slowly, so that we give System 2 a chance to work. The more quickly we have to make a judgement, the more likely it is that we will use System 1. By using System 2 instead, we can evaluate our beliefs more consciously and objectively and need not get tied up in prejudices or incorrect conclusions. Kahneman's behavioural economics model demonstrates one line of thinking about conscious and unconscious decisions.

Somewhat simplistically, we might say that research on the brain concludes that our habits create lasting patterns in the brain. This means that patterns for new habits are deposited on top of old ones, but the original habits do not disappear as they are left to lie dormant. When we encounter sufficiently powerful triggers, the old habits can be brought back to life to take over from the new habits. Should we prefer to keep the new habit, the collaboration between our different brain functions then has a significant challenge to overcome.

This book is about gaining a greater understanding of, and knowledge about, how intrapreneurs and intrapreneurship work. At the same time, positivity, the brain, habitual thinking patterns, decision-making, willpower and patience will be of interest to anyone who wants to become more aware of what governs our choices and decisions.

Also of interest is how and in what way we humans are conscious of our attitudes and approaches and what that means for our ability to communicate with others. If we want to bring about change, we need to reach those people who work in a different way to us and gain a better understanding of conscious and unconscious attitudes.

Conscious and unconscious attitudes

From a psychological perspective, our behaviour is controlled by our conscious or unconscious choices of approach and attitude. We all react to change differently depending on our basic approach to life and what drives us, and these factors in turn influence our attitude and approach at any given moment. One of the challenges for science, and a major point of controversy since time immemorial, is the question of free will and the workings of the conscious and unconscious self.

Our attitudes are crucial to the way we view and communicate with each other, and they influence what we feel about change and development. Various schools of philosophy and psychology have completely different opinions about how human consciousness and free will function and are controlled. I provide an overview of the research and the psychological orientations that are important in terms of how and if we choose to view consciousness as a relevant concept. This takes the form of a summary of some common psychological orientations, i.e. cognitive, psychodynamic and behavioural psychology. I also touch upon biological psychology, which is an interdisciplinary area of knowledge that provides explanations for behaviours, thoughts and emotions in physiological processes and the nervous system. This in turn relates to clinical neuropsychology, which we looked at earlier, and which deals with behaviours and the brain.

One psychological orientation that has been dominant in recent decades, in Sweden at least, is *cognitive psychology*, which is based on how people think and interpret sensory perceptions. It suggests that the way people react is influenced by the way they think, not by external circumstances. It is thought that each individual develops their own personal cognitive schemas, which are organised patterns of thought and behaviour. The individual uses these to understand and react to their experiences. Because these schemas are strongly linked to the individual's identity, it is difficult to change them, although change can take place as a result of new experiences.

In cognitive psychology, the unconscious is not something we have repressed but something we do not register. The opposite to the unconscious is, then, the conscious, what we pay attention to. Some cognitive psychologists believe that our observations are controlled by fundamental beliefs, creating a kind of psychological conservatism. The cognitive schema contains beliefs that are constantly repeated and confirmed through observations. This means that things that are not observed cannot be noted and confirmed. Critics claim that the cognitive perspective places too much importance on people's thinking and neglects their behaviour. In their view, correct thinking does not automatically lead to correct conduct.

Psychodynamic psychology is based on the theories of Freud; it studies our unconscious processes to make us aware of why we behave as we do. There is a great emphasis on the idea of the unconscious person being controlled by conflicting forces in their psyche. Conflicts arise at an early stage in life, when a small child wants to indulge her instincts and fulfil her innate needs while the community around her demands that she puts them aside for the good of society.

Critics say that there is insufficient scientific evidence for the generalisations put forward, and that the focus is on the cause of the problem rather than on the symptoms; this does not help the individual to come to terms with the problem. There is also a question as to whether studies of people with psychological problems can be turned into theories about healthy people.

Behavioural psychology is not relevant to the debate about consciousness and free will. It takes a concrete, practical approach that focuses on observable behaviours and avoids questions of feelings and inner experiences. At its root is the idea that people are conditioned by their environment and personal experiences, and it focuses on how people learn. From this point of view, all behaviours are learned, and if something is wrong we simply need to relearn it. It is based on scientific studies in a laboratory environment. Critics question if it is appropriate to draw direct parallels between animals and people and whether it is right to disregard people's thoughts and emotions. With neurological research having advanced hugely in the last five years, there has been a recent focus on studies looking at the importance of the brain for consciousness. In *neuropsychology*, there have been experiments that some researchers say prove that humans have no free will. They claim that we are controlled by signals from the brain that we have no influence over.

Neuropsychology was one of the interests of researcher and Nobel laureate Francis Crick. In the 1950s, he discovered the structure of the DNA molecule and worked on breaking the genetic code in the human gene pool. He recounts his deterministic view of consciousness in his book *The Astonishing Hypothesis* (1994), in which he claims: "'You', your joys, your memories and your ambitions, your sense of personal identity and free will are in fact no more than the behavior of a vast assembly of nerve cells and their associated molecules." The great illusion, he says, is not our experience of thinking, as that is real enough. Instead, the illusion is the very idea that our thoughts can influence the world around us, that any effort is in any way important and that we have any kind of free will.

Crick collaborated with Professor Christof Koch (1990), who is still active in research. Koch (2014) represents the branch of neuroscientific research that is entirely based on laboratory experimentation and facts. His research looks at how conscious physical experiences can lead to activity in the brain and how physical experiences give rise to non-physical, subjective, conscious states. For him, consciousness is as much a fundamental quality as time, space, energy and mass.

In Koch's opinion, a characteristic feature of conscious experiences is that they are incredibly complex. Every experience contains an enormous amount of information. At the same time, they seem to be constantly joined together in one whole. The use of techniques such as MRI scanning has enabled researchers to begin to map the location of consciousness in the brain, and the part of the brain thought to be behind our conscious experiences includes the cerebral cortex and the thalamus, a sort of "switching station" for sensations in the midbrain.

How important is consciousness for intrapreneurship?

Several of the intrapreneurs interviewed see clear links between the fact that they were unaware that they were intrapreneurs and what has subsequently happened to them individually and in their surroundings in various situations.

For me, a particularly interesting place to start is people's very different reactions to change, depending on their basic attitude to life and what motivates them personally. An individual's behaviour in different situations is influenced by their conscious or unconscious choice of approach and attitude at a given moment.

We can define being conscious as having knowledge, awareness and/or insight. One definition of consciousness is having an in-depth knowledge of oneself and, to an extent, an understanding of one's surroundings. This means both knowledge and an understanding of how our own thoughts and feelings affect us and our behaviour and also being able to answer questions such as, "Who am I?", "What am I thinking about?", and "What is it that I am experiencing and what is its significance for me?" Consciousness also means understanding how we influence others and how they in turn influence us. This means that we reflect on the thoughts, feelings and behaviour of other people, both those in our immediate circles and in society as a whole.

The opposite of consciousness is unconsciousness, which is when we do something without thinking about it. It means we do not understand what we are doing or how it affects both ourselves and others. Making a conscious decision means that we first think through the implications of the decision and the consequences it may have. Doing something unconsciously means doing something without being aware that we are doing it, without thinking about it and without knowing about it. Sometimes we become aware of the things we are doing unconsciously, either at the time or subsequently. When this happens, we may unconsciously want to make it seem that we have made a conscious decision by rationalising our thoughts, feelings and behaviour after the event. By increasing our understanding of how we influence, and are influenced by, our surroundings, we can motivate ourselves to change our approach and adopt a more successful attitude.

One important question is how the interplay between different approaches influences the function of change; there are different parts to our existence, and several processes run in parallel in our lives, in a way that is common to us all.

Another question is how the interaction between different approaches influences individuals, groups and organisations. Encounters between people with similar or different motivations can produce tensions, which can be positive or negative. The interaction that results from this creates the necessary conditions for change. One example of a fundamental difference is that some individuals need a high degree of autonomy, while others prefer to work as part of a team. And some individuals or teams want to be able to adhere to clear rules and regulations, while others require a more autonomous and innovative way of working.

There are models describing how to consciously choose attitudes that make it easier for us to deal with ongoing change by providing greater personal/inner security and a language that expresses our various emotional states and those of others. As a result, we become more secure, understand ourselves better and acquire tools with which to communicate effectively with others.

We can increase the chances of successfully bringing about change by developing a more positive attitude. A greater number of positive experiences or moments makes it possible to choose attitudes and approaches that favour change. We can develop our own awareness of different approaches and attitudes by:

' getting to know ourselves, our needs and our motivations and expressing these in words

' analysing our current situation and setting goals for where we want to be

' identifying a way in which we can personally increase the number of positive experiences we have

- learning how our own mode of communication affects others with either similar or different motivations/approaches, and
- communicating effectively with others using a coaching approach

Changing negative attitudes

Placing an emphasis on personal management, a conscious choice of attitude, positivity and a coaching approach as factors crucial to innovation may strike some people as strange. I have met people who think that positivity in particular is naive and unscientific, and some people are opposed to the whole concept because they feel it is woolly.

I personally believe that these are the cornerstones of good corporate culture. Positivity is actually quite a simple and logical idea if you consider how people function both physically and mentally. For example, looking at it from the point of view of our fundamental needs, we might note that as humans we all endeavour to mobilise our dopamine or other brain substances that help us to feel good. We can do this with the assistance of experiences, sex, food, alcohol and drugs, which, in the right quantities, provide stimulation and a sense of well-being but which have the opposite effect when taken to excess. Since it then becomes a habit, if we want the same kick that we got the first time round we have to gradually increase the dose.

There are similarities between this type of stimulation and the stimulation we get through a positive approach. When we stimulate ourselves using positive emotions, we are, again, activating our dopamine and our endorphins. We can do this by making use of those moments when we feel happiness, hope, inspiration, pride or love, for example, and cultivating the emotions that arise from the experience in a positive way by "returning to them" in our thoughts. The great thing about positivity is that this sort of stimulation does not just have a physical and psychological effect on *us*; our positive frame of mind will also "infect" others. This creates a very special kind of energy and receptiveness that has benefits to both you and those around you – additional strength, new ideas and, last but by no means least, greater resilience in the face of adversity.

This is something we need, as almost all change encounters opposition in some form. Not from everyone, but from a few. It is often those who are the most negative whose voices are heard most. The fact is that, whether you are an intrapreneur, a manager or both, you will find it difficult to get through to all your co-workers, colleagues and managers with your ideas and visions because many of them do not want to change either themselves or their situation. You will undoubtedly encounter these constant naysayers, and will need to live and deal with the fact that you have them around you. These are people who do not want change but who will question you, be jealous of your ideas or be keen to wield power – or they may simply be genuinely convinced that what you stand for is wrong. For whatever reason, you will have people around you who act negatively; people who do not want to change anything, or are not interested in change, because they benefit from the current situation.

If people simply cannot agree what reality might look like or how to get there, an open dialogue about values, visions and short and long-goals usually results in a way forward. In other cases, it is more a question of what is going on in the head of the negative person and what their personal goals are. One of the biggest wins for this type of person is if they can use their negativity to block change, so that they can continue to enjoy the security of their familiar surroundings. Another plus point for them might be to prevent anyone else getting attention or acknowledgement, as it can feel demeaning for people who do not expect to get such attention themselves. Last but not least, there is a kind of power to be had from constantly and openly being contrary and critical of other people. Because negativity is infectious, negative people get confirmation from others that they are "thinking correctly" and are interesting people.

Everyone has the right to their own opinion, but it is hardly productive if an organisation or a company has to call a halt to essential development and change because it is unable to deal with negative attitudes. What happens then is that momentum slows, the energy is lost, there is increased suspicion, everyone is on their guard and creativity declines. But what can be done to reduce the benefits to an individual of negativity? In my experience, the most effective countermeasure is to help people to develop their personal management skills and make it easier for them to make conscious choices of attitude. Once they have the advantage of greater self-awareness and more knowledge of their own unconscious attitudes, many people choose to change in a positive direction.

A combination of group pressure, enticement and stimulating people's curiosity can also help, as can increasing a person's sense of security by giving due attention to all successes, however minor. It is important to notice and affirm good behaviour and not to react to (or punish!) undesirable, less productive behaviour, as any response from you in your capacity as a manager will be an affirmation.

You can also use various catalysts to release tensions within the group and open the door to discussions about shared group rules. An intrapreneur may find it difficult to set their own boundaries and may need support, or may need to seek help from the group if things seem in danger of going adrift. Things *will* go adrift if a person, inside or outside the group, is allowed to get the upper hand with their negative behaviour, stifling everyone else like a wet blanket.

It will of course be much more difficult if the person with a negative attitude is a senior manager who cannot be persuaded to change their thinking. In such cases, it is important, as always, that the intrapreneur gets the support of a protector at the top of the organisation to ensure their project's success. Because it *is* often possible to make people change their attitude, as long as you treat them with respect and employ a listening – i.e., a coaching – approach.

Communication and coaching approaches

It is not possible to force someone to understand what you mean when you say it just because you want them to, as communication always takes place on the recipient's terms. People communicate and interpret each other's messages in different ways – we have different "communication styles". Many organisations use tests that map out and describe their co-workers' communication styles. These aim to provide a better understanding of how a person around us prefers to be addressed and what type of communication they themselves use with others.

The ability to communicate is crucial for establishing a climate of trust. Getting to know yourself in depth, becoming aware of your attitudes and identifying the communication style you yourself prefer makes it easier to find ways to communicate with others. This can help us understand why we may find it difficult to take on board what others say, and also enable us to choose to adapt our communication style to that of others so as to get our messages heard.

A coaching approach is based on creating a sense of trust between people who communicate with each other. What this means is that someone who wants to convey something to someone else must believe in the other person's ability and be interested in that person's reaction and response. We cannot create trust by saying "You can trust me ..." to someone else; trust is something we demonstrate with our actions. It is important to be genuine and not pretend to be someone we are not, and also to be competent, honest and keep promises. Only then can we gain other people's trust.

Communicating using a coaching approach is based on active listening and respect. The conversation technique includes being present in the conversation and adapting your posture, eye contact and attitude and the speed and volume at which you speak to the person you are talking to.

Trust and understanding are crucial

When you meet someone for the first time, either in person or when you read their book, article or blog or listen to them speak, you immediately develop a perception of that person – a first impression that you then take away with you. It is part of our natural instincts when we meet other people to quickly look for something we recognise, something familiar, while at the same time noting differences. The more we recognise in that other person, the more easily we will feel a sense of connection and acceptance with them and the more secure we will feel.

In any encounter with something new, whether a new situation or a new person, there is always a threshold. Even though we are all different as human beings, there are similarities that manifest themselves in different ways. The way we put things into words, our environment and the social rules we have learned all contribute to a sort of "language". When we share that language with someone else, it is easier to get over the threshold and start to get to know one another at a more in-depth level. Failure to get over the threshold can result in mistrust and lead us to question the other person. This is because we use ourselves as a frame of reference in our interactions with others and when we are assessing the correct approach or attitude to a situation. If someone behaves substantially different from us, it is very likely that we will instinctively dismiss that person because their attitude is "wrong".

Each of us has a different threshold, and we need to be able to get over it in order to build trust with the people we meet. Mutual trust is essential if we are to have the confidence to communicate openly and without prejudice and embrace other people's thinking. It determines whether or not we feel we can rely on the other person. However, there are further aspects of our attitudes and approaches that are significant for our understanding of differences, motivations and qualities. Psychologist Claes Janssen sheds light on these different dimensions in his research, and they form the basis of his "Outsider Scale". This is a psychological test that was launched in 1975 and is still used in many countries today.

By using the Outsider Scale, we can achieve a more in-depth understanding of people's fundamental differences and how these in turn affect, for example, the ability of managers to manage themselves and others – something that can be a crucial factor in the success or otherwise of intrapreneurship and innovation.

The Outsider Scale

The central concept in the Outsider Scale is "self-censorship", and the test measures "an individual's willingness or unwillingness to censor themselves and their needs, censor other people, censor the situation around themselves or censor social circumstances."

Janssen's models emerged from a study he undertook during the 1970s of people's attitudes to film censorship. The study asked whether censorship should be retained or removed. During the study, he noticed a pattern amongst the test subjects who were in favour of censorship in that they shared other clear values. The same was true of those who were against censorship, and the results of the study led Janssen to produce the Outsider Scale.

The Outsider Scale asks respondents 24 questions, and their answers are used to place the person on a scale between 0 and 24. The questions are about what people feel and how they view themselves and others in various contexts and must be answered 'Yes' or 'No'. Respondents who answer 'No' to all questions are given a score of 0 while those who answer 'Yes' to all the questions get a score of 24. This means that the scores of 0 and 24 are at the opposite extremes in terms of responses to the questions. The Outsider Scale has been used in much the same way ever since 1975, and many thousands of people in Sweden and other countries have answered the questions. The results show that the responses follow a normal distribution, with the majority of participants around the mean score of 12, with fewer and fewer people the further out on the scale you go in both directions.

Typical 'No' responders, whose scores are between 0 and 11, are people who are more in favour of all types of censorship. The lower a person's score on the scale, the greater their wish for censorship. Janssen's analysis showed that these are people with conventional values and a more traditional approach to themselves, life and society. Those who answered overwhelmingly positively – the 'Yes' responders, with scores of 12 and over – are more distinctive and have an increasingly questioning and unconventional approach and lifestyle the higher their score. The differences between the 'No' and 'Yes' responders increase markedly the further out on the scale their scores. Janssen draws the conclusion that people a long way away from each other on the scale have such widely differing approaches to life that they cannot understand each other's values. As a result, they find it difficult to communicate with each other.

Because the responses follow the normal distribution, this means in practice that both groups are equal in size and that there are equal numbers of 'No' and 'Yes' responders. However, the study shows that when you ask the participants which are in the majority, both 'No' and 'Yes' responders believe that there are many more 'No' responders in society. The general perception is that the 'Yes' responders are in a minority.

This finding leads Janssen to extend his interpretation of the Outsider Scale. He believes that it is the 'No' responders who are traditionally in charge of our social norms and that many 'Yes' responders struggle to adapt themselves to these norms. Other 'Yes' responders choose instead to go their own way, which means that they have to bear the consequences of opting out of the circumstances that prevail in their social set-up, their family, their organisation or their community.

Janssen's conclusion is that the two different approaches to life are a decisive factor in the inability of certain individuals to engage with each other at all. They are so far removed from one another that they simply have no understanding of the way the other person expresses themselves or the positions they take. He believes that a distance of three points between individuals on the Outsider Scale is sufficient for them to have difficulty trusting one another. The further apart two individuals are on the scale, the less likely it is that they will understand one another, which may in turn result in mistrust and uncertainty between the two.

A further aspect of the study is Janssen's measurement of the extent to which a 'Yes' responder is "integrated" or "unintegrated". He investigates how far an individual's life choices are controlled by their personality and how much energy the 'Yes' responder expends in trying to adapt themselves to the attitudes and values that the majority of us perceive as the norm. The more a 'Yes' responder feels that they need to adapt themselves to values that they do not actually share, the more energy that person uses up. The more integrated they are, the more inclined they are to understand both sides, and integration seems to have a greater and more obvious importance the more 'Yes' answers a person gives. Because people further down on the scale answer 'Yes' less often, it may be easier for someone with a score of 12 to be integrated than someone who has scored 24. This means that it may be easier for a person with a score of 12 to feel content than someone who has answered 'Yes' throughout.

Janssen claims that the typical entrepreneur sits somewhere at the edges of the scale, around the 24 mark, and also that earlier tests have shown that a high score on the Outsider Scale correlates with a high level of personal creativity. What might the significance of these scores on the Outsider Scale be for successful intrapreneurship? After all, researchers would suggest that the facts that intrapreneurs are seldom content but rather aspire to change, and that they are also very creative people, are accepted truths.

By way of comparison, Jansson indicates that the normal distribution of Swedish managers on the scale is between 6 and 11. In more conservative sectors such as banking and insurance, the average for managers is lower than that of managers in sectors such as those involving fast-moving consumer goods or the telecoms industry.

The logical conclusion ought to be that there will be a basic low level of trust between traditional managers and intrapreneurs and/or entrepreneurs from the outset and therefore also a difficulty in communicating. As a result there is a sort of mental threshold that has to be crossed before people can work with each other effectively. This is where awareness and knowledge of our differences and values can play a major role in creating a work climate that favours successful innovation.

I myself worked for many years in a conventional and traditionally conservative sector. When I took the Outsider Scale test five years ago for the first time, I got a relatively high score. I would think that when I was young and more radical in my thoughts and actions than I am now my score would have been even higher. (Janssen says that people do not move more than a couple of points on the scale during the course of their lives, unless something significant happens to entirely change their circumstances.) Given that we were probably on opposite ends of the scale, that might explain why I and some of my managers sometimes found it hard to muster the necessary confidence in one another and to develop mutual trust. This became particularly apparent in situations when we were under pressure.

Greater awareness and knowledge about each other's differences and what the consequences of these differences might be can help to increase a person's sense of security and thus engender trust. This is essential if managers in traditional organisations are to have the courage to invest in intrapreneurs whose personality profile is completely different to their own. What makes the Outsider Scale so interesting is that it provides more in-depth insights into how and why we find it so much easier to understand some people than others and so establish differing degrees of trust. It is probably rather difficult to have confidence in another person whose values are completely different to our own. It is even more difficult if we are not aware of, or cannot put into words, the reasons why we feel uncomfortable. Quite simply, we cannot communicate successfully with one another as we do not understand one another's language. And perhaps we do not even understand ourselves.

It is neither possible nor desirable to try to change someone other than ourselves, but, with increased awareness, we can more easily take control of the effect we have on our environment and thus influence the people around us.

The next section looks at various types of obstacles that can hinder or even prevent intrapreneurship and innovation in companies and organisations. I also address the issue of intrapreneurs working alongside entrepreneurs and look at the particular difficulties such situations can present.

CHAPTER 4

BARRIERS TO INTRAPRENEURSHIP

Intrapreneurs are driven by ideas and opportunities, by the belief that there are always things that can be done better, things that can solve problems and enhance performance. Intrapreneurs have ideas and visions for how something might be, and can be frustrated and feel constrained if they come up against barriers such as:

' Negative attitudes from the people around them
' Rules and formalities that hold processes up
' Restrictions that mean the results are not as good as the vision promised

Barriers to innovation can arise from the attitude of individuals or may be in the form of structural and cultural obstacles within the organisation.

A catalyst for disturbing contentment!

An intrapreneur disturbs the sense of contentment within an organisation. As described in the section "Contradiction and difference", the intrapreneur can bring about feelings of insecurity in managers and co-workers who perhaps:

' Have only a short-term focus themselves
' Believe that clear structures and orderliness should be the basis of all activity
' Are content with things that actually work and sell, so wonder why should they change them
' Prioritise limited profit here and now above potentially greater, but uncertain, income in the future
' Do not appreciate people showing their feelings and frustrations openly
' Are risk-averse and want guarantees that outcomes will be positive before entering into a new area

These are the people in the organisation who think it is best to be content with what currently works, who feel that they represent that which is normal, realistic and tested in contrast to those who question the status quo. These conflicts of interest between individuals help to create opposition and barriers between those who are in favour of major changes in the organisation and those who are against. Since such conflicts cannot be avoided if there is a desire to innovate, I like to see the role of the intrapreneur as being a sort of "catalyst for disturbing contentment" in the organisation.

Strategic and cultural barriers

There are, of course, many different reasons why the outcome of a project within an organisation may not be what people believed and hoped it would be. As previously mentioned, researchers feel, and I concur, that certain conditions must be in place in an organisation for intrapreneurship and innovation to be wholly successful. In addition, senior management must be aware of the necessary conditions and what they mean in practice, and must also be aware of the importance of management. Otherwise, an organisation may not even realise what development opportunities it will miss out on if management does the wrong thing or does nothing at all.

Barriers to intrapreneurship and innovation begin at the highest, strategic level. Are innovation and intrapreneurship on management agendas and are they regularly discussed? It is, of course, essential that someone in management is able to act as the sponsor or protector of the intrapreneur. Another crucial strategic issue is the organisation's view of the future and if the owners, board and/or management take a short-term approach to profitability and efficiency. Many companies produce a detailed budget for one year at a time and a strategic plan that runs over five years. The latter often has the same starting point as the budget in terms of product range, services, customer offers and target groups, but provides a somewhat more abstract overview.

Extrapolating from the current situation to five years ahead does not make assessments about the future any more "true" as a basis for decisions or investment than anything felt to be a pure guess, but it can feel safer and more substantiated. However, it can be a problem if it provides a false sense of security that prevents management from being open to information about events in the outside world and from dealing with the ideas and suggestions created within the organisation. This is something that can have a major impact on the organisation over time.

Professor Gautam Ahuja and Curba Morris Lampert (2001) describe various types of restrictions on innovation in technology companies. They believe that these companies have a tendency to fall into a trap and invest in mature technologies, instead of recently-developed technologies, and in solutions that are similar to tried-and-tested ones because they are afraid of taking risks. They claim that it is only by experimenting with technologies that are completely new to the company, or relatively new, emerging, industry-related technologies, that this trap can be avoided. In their opinion, the lack of reward for successful new ideas combined with negative consequences in the event of failure is the fundamental reason why many large companies do not produce revolutionary new solutions despite their substantial resources.

Although opposition to risk-taking can exist at all levels in the organisation, it is most serious when the opposition is at the strategic level. As previously mentioned, it is particularly difficult for co-workers to be open to ideas and innovation if they sense conflicting signals coming from management, i.e. if someone says one thing but then either does the opposite themselves or encourages co-workers who contradict the official line. Or, worse, punishes those who remain on message. Of most significance is management's attitude to risk, as most innovatory projects are subject to some risk-taking and there are no guarantees of success. If an intrapreneur gets into trouble through a mistake or failure, all innovation within the company will be reined in. Failure should instead be seen as a natural part of innovation, and it is also important for management to be encouraging if the innovation is not very successful.

Another strategic approach that can make innovation difficult is the aim to make efficiency gains by outsourcing those skills not seen as core. In their efforts to be ever more cost effective, many companies choose to dismantle their own support functions and to buy in external services in areas such as finance, administration and IT. That makes it very much more difficult to develop cross-functional skills using co-workers who truly master all aspects of the organisation. Consequently, forming powerful intrapreneurial teams to work on innovation can be a more complex process.

Professor Thomas Kalling (2007) is often referenced in respect of identifying barriers to innovation in companies and other organisations. He believes that studying the barriers within organisations makes it easier to understand what the drivers of innovation are. In Kalling's view, it is only human to be attracted more by what is familiar than what is unknown so that we can avoid uncertainty and financial risk. In a study, he identified a number of inbuilt barriers to innovation that show that some organisations may choose, either implicitly or explicitly, not to drive learning and innovation. Instead, they focus on their day-to-day core activity, follow existing procedures and cling to old mindsets.

The study is based on interviews with managers at different levels, innovation specialists and co-workers at a major Swedish industrial company. The employees were asked to answer questions about whether they had worked on innovation and what they had felt about the work climate in a number of successful and unsuccessful innovatory projects. Kalling notes that there are certain established, institutional factors that affect companies at various levels. These interact and subsequently have an impact on learning and the organisational context and thus on the ability to innovate. The three factors he has identified relate to the environment, strategies and visions as well as to guiding principles and values. The study presents a number of barriers to innovation that can be linked to their respective factors. These are:

1. The environment (i.e. the company's customers, competitors and suppliers):
   - The company is not affected by its competitors; it is a mature organisation that competes on economies of scale and price
   - It is dependent on the customer taking the initiative on development; it is not proactive itself
   - Suppliers are small and squeezed on price; they are not partners

2. The company's strategies and visions:
   - The company's vision does not mention innovation
   - There is poor communication between the different levels in the company

3. Internal guiding principles and values that affect the individual:
   - Guiding principles are based on consistency, concentration, tradition, short-term results and risk aversion

- There is no strategy for innovation, nor any resources
- Learning and innovation are not part of the norm
- There is no reward or acknowledgement for those who drive innovation

Kalling says that it is also important to have an understanding of the organisational context and the extent to which it favours or hinders innovation. In three areas – the hierarchical organisation, research and development (R&D), and financing – he identifies critical barriers to an innovative climate in the companies he studied. These are:

1. A strongly decentralised hierarchical organisational structure, with individual profit centres, short-term control mechanisms, limited resources and a lack of interest in innovation

2. An R&D unit that is geographically far removed from the production side, has no communication with the rest of the organisation and focuses on emergency ad hoc solutions and technical problems rather than on business development

3. Financing controlled by long-winded, rigid procedures, limited availability of resources, a lack of slack for employees, and managers unwilling to take risks and lacking in skills

Kalling gives examples of obstacles that arise when innovation is not actually on the management agenda or when there is a complete lack of innovation strategy. It may also be the case that co-workers do not think the strategy is credible or that innovation is not discussed at all lower down in the organisation. Because it is middle managers who are responsible for driving innovative ideas up through the organisation, it is particularly problematic if they are lacking in innovation skills themselves.

Geographical considerations also influence the ability to innovate. One obstacle may be separated working groups or substantial physical distances between R&D and the rest of the organisation. This creates difficulties in respect of cross-functional collaboration and the information-sharing that is essential for innovation.

Kalling uses the expression "slack resources" to mean a worker's own time that is not already allocated to activities such as meetings or actual work tasks. It corresponds to the concept of "idea time" that Göran Ekvall uses when discussing creativity levels in organisations. The lack of slack resources makes it difficult for co-workers both in R&D and in the rest of the organisation to think outside their given terms of reference.

An additional obstacle might be if there are no – or only limited – financial resources allocated to innovation, as the projects may then be hampered by competition for funding. Aside from purely financial limitations, the limited resources provided might be due to a lack of interest in change and innovation. It might also be a case of top management or middle managers demonstrating their unwillingness to take financial risks. Kalling highlights the importance of the institutional factors and the organisational context when management decides to change or introduce a new innovation strategy. It can be a challenge to "pull up the roots", as Kalling puts it, to prevent old organisational structures, control mechanisms, R&D activity, financial procedures, available resources etc. from obstructing the new innovation strategy. He says that a company that does not perceive any external threats, does not get directives from above and is not driven by change, is unlikely to:

· Allocate resources
· Change structures, control or financial procedures
· Increase R&D activity
· Link R&D with the main organisation
· Stimulate a broadening of the knowledge base
· Drive knowledge sharing

Neither is it likely that other measures needed to ensure the success of the new innovation strategy will be put in place. Kalling notes that learning and innovation are not solely dependent on ability – they are also dependent on will. In practice, if there is no will, there will be no change, a conclusion that is confirmed by a study from the University of Gothenburg, Sweden.

How a manager's attitude can obstruct innovation

There is no doubt that managers are key to whether or not an intrapreneur is successful. This means that their assessment of the innovation climate and the barriers they perceive in the organisation is crucial. Researcher Leif Denti specialises in the psychology of innovation. He and journalist Martin Kreuger worked together on a study for the Swedish magazine *Chef [Leadership]* (2015) on barriers to innovation in the public sector. Around 1,200 managers took part in the study, during which they were asked to state their position on seven different attitudes that can obstruct innovation in the workplace.

In general, the managers were positive about change and their own innovative ability. However, there was a significant difference between top managers and middle managers, in that the former were considerably more positive about their own abilities than the latter. The researchers concluded that the views of the middle managers were affected by the fact that they had less flexibility in terms of their actions and budgets. The managers' responses were correlated with an estimation of their own ability to innovate, and attitudes that obstructed innovation were ranked as follows:

- We can't
- We don't want to
- We aren't allowed to
- We don't need to
- We can't afford to
- We don't dare to
  We haven't got time (not statistically significant)

The results showed that by far the most significant attitudes obstructing innovation were, as the managers saw it, "we can't" and "we don't want to". The greatest obstacle proved to be a lack of knowledge and ideas about how to bring about change. The next most important was the manager's perception that co-workers were not interested or willing to engage in work on change. A lack of time and resources is seen as a brake on development yet is the least important factor in managers' assessments of their ability to innovate.

In their analysis of the responses to the survey, the researchers note that the managers can be helped to feel better about innovation if given more knowledge. They suggest training on how to cultivate new ideas, clear the ground for their co-workers, turn chaos into something positive and prioritise work on innovation. Co-workers who are reluctant to get involved can be persuaded to engage, say the researchers, if their motivation can be strengthened. One way to do this is to give them the authority to implement innovations and ensure that there are no negative consequences if they are unsuccessful.

Intrapreneurs have a unique ability to operate even in an atmosphere of distrust where their ideas are being questioned, provided resistance is not too fierce. Isabel Engberg and Sara Lundström (2014) show in a dissertation how intrapreneurs create an intrapreneurial context around themselves whether or not there has been any energy around innovation in the organisation previously. If faced with significant opposition over a longer period, an intrapreneur will close down their projects, move to another employer or set up their own business.

Other cultural barriers

Several researchers have noted that one obstacle to innovation might be that the intrapreneur is not acknowledged in large organisations because they do not behave in the way the company expects. Researchers Nupur Sinha and Kailash B. L. Srivastava (2013) demonstrate in their studies that a significant obstacle to a company's development of innovative ability is a lack of the socio-cultural factors that allow for the individualism and low power distance essential for intrapreneurship. The extent to which intrapreneurship is viewed in a positive light can be directly linked to the degree to which individuals are able to be outward-looking in their work, get intellectual stimulation and have an outlet for their creativity. Their research shows the particular characteristics of intrapreneurs to be that they are outward-looking, unselfish, creative and performance-oriented. The researchers' conclusion is that companies that want to influence their own ability to innovate need to become aware of, and adapt to, these conditions, manage recruitment and invest in ongoing training.

Intrapreneurs in small organisations

Researchers often make the assumption that intrapreneurs work only in large, established companies and organisations. But of course there *are* examples of intrapreneurs going into small companies and working alongside the entrepreneur who originally set up the business. An entrepreneur collaborating with an intrapreneur makes for a very special situation and dynamic, which is the subject of this section. The discussion requires a broader definition of the concept of the entrepreneur than has been employed previously in this book.

Researchers define an entrepreneur as a person who starts up a completely new business or someone who is still leading a company that they started just over three years ago (this is the basis of the GEM study). After that, the company is deemed to be an established firm irrespective of size. That distinction is important when entrepreneurship is analysed from the point of view of innovation. However, in everyday speech we like to use the term "entrepreneur" to describe any person who has set up their own business. This is irrespective of whether the company has subsequently developed into a small but established firm or gone on to be what is known as a growth company, increasing its turnover substantially year on year. It is also important to note that not all small business owners started out as entrepreneurs; some do not have entrepreneurial drive and run their own businesses simply to earn a living.

Whatever the reason, many entrepreneur-run companies arrive at a point where the person who started them needs additional human resources. The company may then employ an intrapreneur in a senior position to work side by side with the original entrepreneur. A collaboration bringing together two strong personalities with both similar and differing motivations is not always straightforward.

As a consultant, I have met several intrapreneurs in that situation, and I also interviewed a number in preparation for this book. Their stories form the basis of the scenarios I describe. This does not mean that their version of events is any truer than the perspective given by the entrepreneur/owner, but the aim of this book is, after all, to develop a greater understanding of the intrapreneurial personality and how it influences and is influenced by its surroundings. There has been a gradual realisation that the way these two personalities combine is of crucial importance. This is borne out by the interview with intrapreneur C, who has been the CEO of an entrepreneurial industrial company for two years.

"I don't see myself as an intrapreneur" – the words of C, someone I have long thought of as having an intrapreneurial personality. He is the CEO of a small, family-owned, entrepreneurial company. Previously, he worked for many years at a large company in the Swedish service sector, for part of that time as the regional manager. C is someone who never seems to sit still. He is always spotting new opportunities and is constantly aiming to change, improve and develop both at work and at home.

"I've met several intrapreneurs at work, and it is incredibly important not to shut them down when they have ideas because they'll stop taking the initiative", he says. "They're restless, in a good way, and have a tendency to get carried away. Their heads are buzzing with ideas and a new one can pop out at any time – which has an impact on day-to-day work", he adds, smiling. After a moment he continues. "You have to create a culture that allows them to do things outside their normal terms of reference. For example, you have to accept that they can't get to meetings on time, keep things in order or submit timesheets. As a manager, you have to have an accommodating approach to the less positive sides of your intrapreneur."

In C's view, what distinguishes organisations that can make the most of their intrapreneurs from those that cannot is their maturity, skills levels and knowledge. If management at the highest level is not receptive, there will not be enough freedom to innovate. It is important to seize hold of ideas rather than kill them off. He refers here to general, positive leadership qualities, and he thinks that both personal management and an understanding of the needs of the individual are important. He says that an intrapreneur must have a high profile in the organisation, and that this is often far more important than financial reward. The very worst thing that can happen is for someone else to take the intrapreneur's idea and make it their own – that will make the intrapreneur down tools and move to a competitor.

C himself is driven by a sense of curiosity, ambition and continuous analysis. He asks himself, "Why we do things this way?", and "Is this right, or can it be done another way?", and he analyses environments, social contexts and the people around him. Seeing the big picture is important, and he is passionate about developing organisations and encouraging other people to develop, even if it is primarily the needs and realities of customers that determine priorities and the choice of projects.

During our conversation it emerges that C has grown tired of having to deal with aversion to change in his current organisation. Although he has great staying power, he finds that when he wants to try out new ideas or methods he is met by too many comments along the lines of "We've tried that before". He stresses that personal development is important and underlines that, in previous roles, he had cross-functional contacts within the organisation. That helped to fulfil his need for social exchange and intellectual stimulation, something he now feels is missing. He would like to see management being more receptive and more open-minded, so that it seizes hold of ideas and makes the most of the drive within the organisation. Research and development are important in any organisation, but they are restricted by financial considerations. Small companies often do not have the funds to invest in the type of development needed for intrapreneurs to grow.

That takes us on to the topic of the relationship between an entrepreneur and an intrapreneur. I ask if he thinks it is difficult for an intrapreneur to enter into an entrepreneurial, or owner-led, company as CEO or manager. "Yes, very much so. You get conflict when the entrepreneur has their own set view of things and is not prepared to change. It's probably quite a common situation, as the entrepreneur has found their niche and got results by stubbornly sticking to their own ideas."

C says that many of today's entrepreneurs have achieved a lot without any special training. Instead, they are incredibly good at what they know and have succeeded in managing and building a business around that. So having someone come in as an intrapreneur does not work; it gives rise to a sort of power struggle. The entrepreneur or owner will be keen to hand over some of their tasks but less interested in listening to ideas about new methods or new ways of working. The issue of least interest to them is finding ways to develop the people working in the business. That, at least, is C's own experience. He notes, "It's probably the same as in so many other situations when an intrapreneur has no outlet for their needs and drive. What happens is that they stop working on their project or move to another organisation."

C is not the only one holding that view. As a consultant, I have worked for a number of different companies owned and run by the entrepreneur who set up the business in the first place. In companies where the entrepreneur is the majority owner and the CEO employed is an intrapreneur, the term "power struggle" seems highly appropriate, and it is an expression used by C in the interview above. What is described is a power struggle that does not always take place openly and where other people sometimes find it difficult to keep up with what is happening.

These troublesome situations arise because entrepreneurs and intrapreneurs have personality traits and motivations in common, although there are also clear differences between them. The strength of their motivation is similar, but their aims differ. In other words, entrepreneurs and intrapreneurs often agree on certain things, but may compete with each other in other respects and sometimes prioritise differently. As long as the entrepreneur owns the company, the entrepreneur makes the decisions, which can be hard for the intrapreneur to appreciate and accept. This means that a business rarely develops exactly as the intrapreneur would like while the entrepreneur remains the majority owner and leads the organisation.

Entrepreneurs who started an innovative business many years ago and who are still majority owners of their businesses have a number of character traits in common. Equally, there are similarities between the intrapreneurs who are employed as CEOs in such companies. I believe the factors below to be the most relevant to the relationship between an entrepreneur and an intrapreneur. (They are partially a restating of the entrepreneur's and intrapreneur's qualities, motivations and behaviours.)

Entrepreneurs:
- focus on their own idea or innovation
- are often very stubborn and driven individuals with the ability to put their ideas into practice
- may be innovative people with new ideas, or
- opposed to change, particularly if it "disrupts" their original idea or innovation (their baby)
- are used to being the centre of attention and making decisions, both because of the authority they have as owner and because they were the originator of the business idea and/or innovation.
- feel secure in their area of knowledge and the field in which they have achieved success
- are able to feel satisfaction when they have achieved success, having seen their idea become a reality
-

- may have blinkers on (in the intrapreneur's view) or take a realistic approach (in the entrepreneur's own view) when it comes to the need to continue developing the company and its workers and the required resources
- may not have the wider set of skills necessary for developing the business
- may find it difficult to hand over control to others

Intrapreneurs:
- are driven by their own visions alongside those of the company
- are driven by development and opportunities and are rarely satisfied
- cannot stay in an environment where there is no freedom
- have very little regard for authority
- focus on the big picture
- are comfortable with constant change
- often have a wide set of skills, develop their co-workers and encourage cross-functional working
- seek out active collaboration with other people who have greater or different skills
- are used to having access to different types of resources

The motivations and behaviours of entrepreneurs and intrapreneurs can lead to conflict between them. The following examples are based on my experiences working as a consultant in entrepreneur-run companies.

Owner/entrepreneur Alex and CEO/intrapreneur Sam

Alex and his late wife had built up a small but very profitable construction group in southern Sweden. After twenty years, profit levels began to decline at the same time as Alex was approaching retirement. Sam, a consultant, had previously had success with an important project at the company, and Alex decided that Sam should succeed him as CEO.

Sam was ambitious in his new CEO role, and his plans included:
- strengthening the brand to attract new customers
- developing new solutions and adapting some existing solutions to sell to new customers or target groups

- creating a more professional organisation with an effective management function and structure

Alex did not really understand Sam's "language", but was attracted by:
- Sam's compelling work on creating an image for the company
- the thought of the company growing more quickly
- the idea of being able to sell the company in the near future

After a while, CEO Sam felt that:
- Alex was refusing to let go of the reins
- none of the senior managers dared to contradict Alex for fear of looking stupid
- His proposed actions and changes were constantly being questioned
- Alex was not sharing his customer contact details with him

Alex gradually felt that:
- Sam was wanting to change things that had been working well for years
- Sam seemed to have his own agenda
- key people were starting to get involved in aspects of the business that were outside their areas of responsibility

For a couple of years, Sam's frustration at what he called Alex's "self-righteous, domineering attitude and need to be in control" grew. He said that Alex was obstructing essential development and having a negative impact on the company's results. Sam came to the conclusion that the management team needed to take action to reduce Alex's influence and/or have Alex removed from the business. Sam's plan was supported by other shareholders, who lobbied the board. But as Alex was the principal and dominant owner, the initiative was, of course, doomed to failure. As the other shareholders were needed for production purposes, they were eventually "forgiven" and allowed to stay, although somewhat crushed. They then put the blame for everything on Sam, who had to leave the company and give up his company shares. A year or two later, the company was sold for a very considerable sum, very largely thanks to Sam's earlier work on strengthening the brand and attracting new client groups.

Another example:

Owner/entrepreneur Kay and CEO/intrapreneur Robyn

Entrepreneur and CEO Kay started the company ten years ago with a unique new service. The company now had around thirty employees and was finding it difficult to remain profitable. At the same time, Kay was being strongly challenged by the employees in her role as CEO because of what they saw as her authoritarian and controlling manner. Her co-workers felt Kay was often unreasonable and negative when it came to developing the company and introducing changes. She kept all the important customer contact details to herself and showed little confidence in the abilities of her co-workers, which did not go down well with new recruits who were young and skilled. In the end, the only way to retain the key people in the company was to make them minority shareholders and also comply with demands that Kay should step down as CEO.

The company took on a new CEO who took a new broom to the administrative and financial procedures but left to take another job within a year. The departing CEO reported that Kay's controlling personality and the fact that she only delegated the more tedious tasks were crucial factors in their decision to leave. The company then decided to take on Robyn, who had previously been CEO in a slightly bigger firm. Robyn immediately set about overhauling sales and the company branding, and started to raise the profile of the company by introducing a new logo and new staff uniforms. Before long, Robyn had signed a contract for new premises and was planning to open a couple of new, local offices in other parts of the country, which would require the hiring of new staff.

Among other things, Robyn wanted to:
- encourage the company's own co-workers and attract customers with a new visual identity
- develop the skills of their co-workers
- allow key people to get involved with product development, mainly new services
- increase upselling, for example of services to existing customers

Kay was attracted by Robyn's:
- wealth of ideas, including the idea of expanding by opening new offices
- new ways of raising the profile of the company
- ability to take the staff along with her and secure their involvement

After a while, Robyn felt that Kay:
- was stubborn, and did not listen to other people
- wanted to keep control of the details, even those relating to finance, sales and product development
- opposed essential changes
- was too cautious in her investments and unwilling to take financial risks

Kay felt after a while that Robyn:
- had big plans that had no basis in reality
- wasted "other people's money" without having control of the company's finances
- wanted to change things that were already working
- was questioning the basis of the business, the new service and the original business concept, and thus Kay herself

Kay was positive about the various initiatives to start with, but eventually she complained about the additional costs. Robyn felt that Kay had become an obstacle to the company's development. The other managers were not brave enough to go against Kay and support the action that needed to be taken as long as Kay remained in a managerial position. Robyn "took hold of the problem" and agreed with Kay that she should leave the management team. They produced a joint plan that set out how Kay would stand down completely within a couple of years. Initially she was on board with the arrangement to hand over the company, but deep down she was annoyed at having been asked to do so.

Before long, Kay found an opportunity to challenge Robyn on a factual basis, saying that Robyn had wasted money the company did not have. As a result, Robyn had to leave the company after less than nine months, and six months later the company had still not recruited a new CEO. One or two key people subsequently left the company, which caused the company severe problems, and production and profitability quickly declined. Two years further on, the company's sales have still not returned to their previous level.

The accounts above support those researchers who claim that successful intrapreneurs are mainly to be found in large companies. These rather conflict-ridden examples clearly show how two personalities that are at the same time very similar and very different can find it difficult to work together. There are of course examples of other partnerships that worked very well once the parties had worked out their respective roles.

In both these cases, the original entrepreneurs are described by both their co-workers and the intrapreneurs as quite authoritarian and controlling. This might be a coincidence, or might be due to the fact that the entrepreneur is now an established company director with a clear status and is used to leading and making decisions. Neither is it surprising if the CEOs/intrapreneurs have a tendency to exaggerate their accounts, as intrapreneurs do react very strongly and negatively to anything they perceive as authoritarian behaviour. However, the intrapreneurs in the examples come across as scheming and manipulative in their efforts to get the entrepreneur to hand over control so that they can implement change.

Even if in these cases what happened in practice was a power struggle, I would suggest that the dramatic turn of events was not due to any intent or ill will but simply down to ignorance. The struggle arose because of the clash of two strong personality types. The entrepreneur and the intrapreneur had similar visions for the business, but their strategies and interim goals were different. Both cases involved people who either had no insight into, or could not deal with, their own basic motivations or those of the other party, especially not those relating to freedom or control.

The question, then, is not what entrepreneur-led companies have to gain by allowing intrapreneurs in, but whether it is possible to create the security, trust and autonomy both parties need to ensure that the intrapreneur's work is a success. Without an understanding of how the interests of the various parties interact with and negate each other, success will be extremely difficult to achieve. If, as in these examples, the situation leads to a power struggle and defensive behaviour, the result will be that the intrapreneur will be the loser in the short term while the business may lose out over time.

It is by no means a disadvantage for a company to be led for a long period by the strong entrepreneur that set it up – in fact the opposite can be true. In the next section, we look at how current research highlights the advantages of strong, forward-looking, innovative entrepreneurs and how they can contribute to continuous innovation. However, not all company directors are innovative by nature, and sooner or later it becomes necessary for even the most innovative entrepreneur to take a back seat. That means it is important to forestall any problems that might arise in connection with a generational shift and take the opportunity to lay the foundations for something new.

In addition, in my experience, if there *is* a CEO that can successfully manoeuvre an entrepreneur out of their own business, it will not be someone with an intrapreneurial personality. Not until a company suffers acute financial problems will the board choose to bypass the principal owner by appointing a new CEO, and what they often look for in that situation is candidates with experience of making cost savings rather than those with experience of development. It might be a sensible use of resources not to wait until there is a financial disaster or leadership crisis but to try to find ways in which the entrepreneur and intrapreneur can learn to derive benefit from one another. With greater understanding of each other's differences and better communication, even small entrepreneur-owned companies should be able to work with an intrapreneur to achieve successful development.

This section of the book has clearly shown that there are obstacles to innovation and intrapreneurship in many different parts of an organisation. They may arise at board level, in the management team or amongst colleagues and co-workers, and come from both individuals and teams. Intrapreneurs may represent obstacles themselves if they lack awareness of "the effect they are having on others".

However, there are companies and organisations that have found ways of overcoming the various obstacles and managed to create the right conditions for innovation and constant renewal. In the next section, I say more about the concept of "continuous innovation" and what researchers claim is essential to enable companies and organisations to survive and achieve long-term success.

CHAPTER 5

THE MEANS TO ACHIEVING SUCCESSFUL INTRAPRENEURSHIP

Continuous innovation in organisations

Increasingly, researchers are claiming that creating the right conditions for radical change in companies and organisations requires completely new organisational structures. Many of them propose concepts such as the "intrapreneur" (or "internal entrepreneur") and "continuous innovation" as essential to success. However, there are differences between the more theoretical views of researchers on what is required to manage innovation and create the right conditions for continuous innovation and the practical attitude of many business leaders. Out in the companies themselves, development is regarded by many people as a means rather than an end, the strongest driver being the need for the core business to grow. So, for corporate management, "innovation" may be more relevant than "intrapreneurship".

Researchers and industry representatives are, however, increasingly in agreement that we are facing a paradigm shift in the way we lead and organise our companies and organisations. The more competitive a market is, the more rapid the changes, but one of the difficulties is knowing whether or not we are, in fact, in a competitive market, since the rapid development of knowledge and information technology is creating opportunities for radical innovation in places where we would least expect it. This is why in the future the knowledge and creativity of our co-workers will be our most important strategic resource. And this means that we need to adapt our leadership and our organisations in line with our increasing dependency on our co-workers' creative capabilities.

The ever-increasing speed of change and the importance of workers' skills for our future are reflected in the Davos World Economic Forum's choice of theme for 2016. That theme was "The Fourth Industrial Revolution", described by the forum's Founder and Executive Chair Klaus Schwab (2016) as follows: "The possibilities of billions of people connected by mobile devices, with unprecedented processing power, storage capacity, and access to knowledge, are unlimited. And these possibilities will be multiplied by emerging technology breakthroughs in fields such as artificial intelligence, robotics, the Internet of Things, autonomous vehicles, 3-D printing, nanotechnology, biotechnology, materials science, energy storage, and quantum computing".

In one of the reports to emerge from the Forum, *The Future of Jobs* (2016), researchers set out what will be required of employees in the future. A survey has been undertaken of how HR managers and strategic directors of global companies view employment, skills and strategies in the context of recruiting labour in the next few years. According to the report, by 2020 the fourth industrial revolution will already have given us advanced robotics and autonomous transport, artificial intelligence and machine learning, advanced materials, biotechnology and genomics (advanced DNA research). Researchers say that this means that around 35% of the capabilities that companies currently ask for in their employees will be different in only a few years' time.

This development will affect both the way we live and the way we work. Some tasks will disappear, the amount of work in other areas will increase and job types that currently do not even exist will become more and more common. What is certain is that the citizens of the future will need to adapt their skills in order to keep up with the demand. According to the report, the employees of the future will need to have a range of different skills, but, when we compare 2020 with 2015, it is in the ranking of these skills that major differences arise.

The skills companies require of their co-workers:

2020	2015
1. Complex Problem Solving	1. Complex Problem Solving
2. Critical Thinking	2. Coordinating with Others
3. Creativity	3. People Management
4. People Management	4. Critical thinking
5. Coordinating with Others	5. Negotiation
6. Emotional Intelligence	6. Quality Control
7. Judgement and Decision Making	7. Service Orientation
8. Service Orientation	8. Judgement and Decision Making
9. Negotiation	9. Active Listening
10. Cognitive Flexibility	10. Creativity

Creativity will be one of the three main skills that co-workers will need to master. With all the new products, new technologies and new ways of working, creativity will be essential if companies are to benefit from the changes.

Capability in quality control and active listening will need to make way for emotional intelligence and cognitive flexibility.

The report concludes that the changes will not wait for us, and so business leaders, teachers and governments all need to be proactive in terms of skills development and re-education so that everyone can benefit from the fourth industrial revolution.

According to Klaus Schwab, businesses will be affected by the fourth industrial revolution in four critical areas: customer expectations, product improvement, innovation and organisational formats. He says that whether the customer is a private individual or a business, the customer experience and the customer's need for service are key. Digital solutions will bring about improvements in both physical products and service, and new forms of cooperation will be needed to cope with fast-moving, radical innovation. Finally, the emergence of global platforms and other new business models means that talent, corporate culture and organisational formats need to be reconsidered.

Where researchers are also in agreement is that there is a difference between successfully leading intrapreneurs and intrapreneurial teams and leading other co-workers and working groups. They also agree that the need for structures and a work climate that support continuous innovation makes demands on the whole organisation. For an organisation to be able to manage its everyday activity alongside innovation there needs to be a consensus, a strategy and knowledge at all levels about what innovation means. That involves everyone from owners and boards, CEOs and management, intrapreneurs and intrapreneurial teams to – last but not least – other managers, colleagues and co-workers in the organisation.

A new management concept for continuous innovation

Researchers are also putting forward ideas about how companies and organisations will need to change in order to be able to cope with the challenges of the future. One of these is the Swedish researcher Annika Steiber, whose focus is on dynamic, innovative organisations.

Steiber spent a year investigating the factors that are key to Google's success and presents her findings in her book *The Google Model - Managing Continuous Innovation in a Rapidly Changing World.* Steiber (2014) summarises what she learned at Google as a number of management principles that she claims are fundamental to the businesses of the future as they will be completely dependent on continuous innovation. A later book, *Silicon Valley Model* (2016), joint authored with Sverker Alänge, is based on these principles and is an analysis of several very well-known, successful companies. The book identifies strong similarities between companies such as Facebook, LinkedIn, Twitter, Tesla Motors and Apigee.

The ability to be continuously innovative is a critical business skill for most companies today, irrespective of sector. Innovation is no longer the remit solely of R&D or product development departments; it has become a strategic responsibility for boards and corporate management. Steiber refers to Schumpeter's theory of the "ongoing creative destruction" in society, which is in turn leading to new and radical innovation. This, along with the accelerating pace of change and globalisation of knowledge, demands change in both leadership and management.

Steiber claims that almost all sectors currently focus far too much on control and quality. This is because many managers lack knowledge of how to go about creating and developing value-adding innovative strategies and revitalized business systems and models. Consequently, it is highly likely that they will continue to use established methods for quality development and efficiency improvements. In Steiber's view, the way to provide the right basis for the necessary change is to shift the focus from traditional management with its specific goals, clear directives and careful monitoring. Instead, management's role should be to identify an overall direction and create opportunities for experimentation. Management should also build knowledge within their organisation and develop their co-workers' motivation by providing them with challenges and stimulating tasks. One obstacle to successful change, however, is limited documented and systematised knowledge of practices that actually work.

Steiber suggests that Google is one of the best examples of how a company can achieve rapid growth while retaining the ability to innovate. What it demonstrates is radical innovation that has brought about sweeping changes and at the same time introduced a whole new set of realities to many different sectors. According to Steiber, the two most important drivers of continuous innovation at Google are the corporative culture and the individuals. Google's corporate culture is based on shared standards and values that in turn stimulate innovation and ongoing improvement. Two examples of this are how the company recruits new co-workers and how it divides up working hours.

Google's employees are described as "generous, open, dedicated people – colleagues with shared expectations". Steiber says that these attitudes create teams that are strongly motivated, and team members endeavour to eliminate anything that gets in the way of innovation. Google invests a good deal of time and money into its recruitment processes and uses its own skilled recruiting staff. One choice the company makes is to recruit only those who share Google's vision and values and are approved by colleagues and co-workers. To enable co-workers to play their part in the company's work on innovation, their working hours are allocated between different activities. According to Steiber, 70% of co-workers' hours are devoted to core activity, 20% to projects related to the core activity, and 10% to other development. She also points out the need for a balance between order and freedom and quotes someone who claims that the Google workplace is 50% structured and 50% chaos.

Steiber highlights Google's management model as being fundamental to the company's success with continuous innovation. The model covers corporate culture, leadership, organisational structure, and value and reward systems. She summarises it as "Google's 10 practices to promote innovation":

1. A challenging and engaging long-term **vision** and **mission**.
2. A management team that **trusts** its employees and has a **passion for innovation** and a focus on continuous change.
3. A strong **innovation-oriented culture** that permeates everything the company does and puts the emphasis on continuous change and innovation, thinking big, speed, collaboration, ethics, putting users first and investing in the right people.
4. **Natural leaders** with the ability to develop successful individuals and teams.
5. A great **belief in individuals** and their capabilities, and substantial investment in the selection process so as to **choose the right people**.
6. A semi-structured, flat, **ambidextrous**, **network-based organisation** with small teams and soft control mechanisms.
7. **Dynamic management systems updated on a quarterly basis** that clarify goals and priorities for all co-workers; fair and transparent **processes for evaluation and promotion** in which the "wisdom of the crowd" has input into evaluation; and company-wide processes for **recognising and rewarding** desirable behaviour.
8. **Fast, iterative learning processes** at both the business level and the product level.
9. Openness to external innovation and an organisation well-integrated into the external environment.
10. A **strong brand** that is associated with innovation.

Most of these points correspond to what we have covered in earlier sections of this book. Here, in principle, is everything needed for the creation of an intrapreneurial culture. Steiber herself claims that Google's management model adheres to certain "organisational laws", and she has chosen to formulate these as "6 management principles for continuous innovation".

The six principles are about the company's ability to *sense and describe threats and opportunities*, to *make the most of opportunities* and, when necessary, to *maintain and regroup the company's resources*. They also refer to the need for proactive work on *continuous renewal* of the business from a holistic perspective.

Steiber stresses the need to set free the inherent innovative energy of every co-worker by creating the right environment. She says that an organisation needs to be *"ambidextrous"* in order to be able to combine its day-to-day work with innovation. There are clear differences here between traditional thinking about planning and control and the need for more freedom, flexibility and willingness to experiment. Organisations must also be, in Steiber's view, *dynamic*, *open* to and *networked* with the world around them and committed to cross-functional cooperation within the organisation, so as to create an environment that can inspire innovation.

For Steiber, her experiences at Google show that the view that only certain people are innovators is an old-fashioned one, and that anyone can be systematically trained in how to innovate. At the same time, she emphasises that there are often a number of individuals in any organisation who are more innovative, or more radically innovative, than others. She therefore suggests that these idea generators are identified, acknowledged and rewarded for their work, thus establishing a kind of hero culture around innovation. Google has chosen to reward teams rather than individuals.

In their later book, *Silicon Valley Model*, Steiber and Alänge (2016) describe how all the companies they studied focus on recruiting what they see as the right kind of people and describe the best co-workers as "a special type". What characterises the best co-workers is that they:

- Are entrepreneurial by nature and passionate about their work
- Are constantly questioning the status quo
- Are individualistic, strong-minded, collaborative and adaptable all at once
- Strive for personal satisfaction, at the same time as they are very committed team players who want to be part of something bigger
- Are clever, enquiring and humble

The writers describe these co-workers as "quite rare and agile in both their thoughts and actions". For me, they have the same complex personality that I have identified myself in the type of co-worker that other researchers call an intrapreneur; the only difference is that the writers use the term "entrepreneur" or "internal entrepreneur" instead.

Google's practices to promote innovation and Steiber's management principles also largely tally with the research into intrapreneurs and intrapreneurship. The concepts used appear both in the research and in the stories of the intrapreneurs themselves – words and expressions such as vision, passion, belief, clear goals, good management, an innovation-friendly culture, knowledge, cross-functional skills, ambidextrous organisations, trust, acknowledgement and reward.

How can businesses get better at continuous innovation? The researchers stress that it is the responsibility of the board and management to take the lead. Steiber suggests that board members, management teams and day-to-day managers should receive special training on the implications of innovation. She claims that the kinds of thought patterns that entrepreneurs have can be taught and that this could make managers better equipped to coach and develop their co-workers in entrepreneurial thinking.

This might seem like an exercise in semantics, simply playing with words. But training in intrapreneurship for owners and managers is an excellent way to help them decide if they and their organisation are ready to invest in innovation and their intrapreneurs. As will be apparent, I do not share Steiber's view that intrapreneurs and entrepreneurs have the same motivations and operate in the same way or that anyone can be an entrepreneur/intrapreneur. Management training in this context should focus on intrapreneurs and intrapreneurship but must also highlight both the similarities and differences between intrapreneurs and entrepreneurs. The research shows that many co-workers are engaged in stepwise, incremental innovation, which they work on as intrapreneurs with management support. However, radical innovation requires the personality of an autonomous intrapreneur.

Another possibility put forward by Steiber is that management starts by establishing a parallel structure in the company to provide direct support to the new way of working. The aim is to avoid innovative ability being "stifled by the way the company currently does things". The parallel structure would be temporary and would be dismantled once the new way of working is sufficiently established to be integrated into the company's core structure. I am in full agreement with this, as it is doubtful whether "incubators" that are set apart from normal operations can be innovative in the long term. The danger is that it will eventually become more difficult for co-workers to get the benefit from the contacts, cross-cutting skills and processes of day-to-day activity. This means they might then miss out on the energy that comes with being part of regular operations. Google's solution involving the allocation of working hours is an interesting alternative.

A further suggestion made by Steiber is that organisations speed up and at the same time safeguard the innovative process by involving senior mentors and colleagues in the evaluation of ideas and prototypes. She also points out, quite rightly, that it is important for senior management to realise and accept that not all projects will be successful and profitable.

This is what I see as one of the most challenging problems for management. It is the responsibility of management to ensure that the intrapreneur's colleagues and mentors are the right people to determine whether projects are credible and worth investing in. At Google and the other Silicon Valley companies, all co-workers are recruited on the basis of a strict assessment that includes innovative ability and shared values. It is difficult, if not virtually impossible, to create that sort of environment in an established company operating along traditional lines. This means that the company may not have the courage to take risks on new ideas, with the result that development is hampered.

Finally, the successful companies highlighted in Steiber and Alänge's analysis have a further interesting factor in common. It transpires that all these companies have/have had founders with strong personalities who have remained in control over a long period. These are entrepreneurs who continue to lead their businesses by means of personality and a strong culture, and their leadership sets its stamp on the companies in spite of their extremely rapid expansion.

These people continue to think and act in accordance with the values that were important to the company when it was set up and, according to the writers, continue to actively oppose bureaucracy, hierarchies and restrictive job descriptions. They say that it is precisely that long-term perspective that has been one of the major success factors for those companies whose founder is still part of the management team, as taking a long-term view creates space for innovation. A long-term perspective can be hard to achieve in companies that operate from quarter to quarter with the associated need to demonstrate constant, short-term improvements in their results. With their analysis of successful, innovation-driven companies, Steiber and Alänge make an interesting and valuable contribution to the debate about how companies and their co-workers can create continuous innovation.

In the next section, "Reflections and Conclusions", I summarise my thinking on the subject of this book. I then round off with some practical recommendations and advice both to management teams and intrapreneurs about issues to be considered when a company appoints, or is planning to appoint, an intrapreneur.

CHAPTER 6

REFLECTIONS AND CONCLUSIONS

Based on research, this book provides an account of thoughts, ideas, knowledge and experiences of intrapreneurship and innovation, some my own and some those of other people. If you are an owner, board member or company director, I have aimed to provide you with the support you need to create the right conditions for successful innovation in your business. I also see the book as a means of sharing expertise and experiences with managers, colleagues and co-workers working alongside one or more intrapreneurs. The book also addresses any intrapreneurs who are looking to become more aware of the effect they have on other people while gaining a greater understanding of how they influence and are influenced by their environment. And because it is about increasing knowledge and understanding of innovation throughout the organisation, it may also provide insights to anyone working in HR, on staffing issues, in organisational or leadership development or in recruitment. You may have an important role to play in recruiting an intrapreneur, which is something I return to in the final chapter in the section on recommendations and advice.

As the book shows, all innovation depends on people thinking outside their normal terms of reference, seeing opportunities and having the courage to try out new things. In essence, it is about creating the conditions and space for individual creativity and intrinsic motivation. This in turn requires a climate of trust and confidence in the workplace in which managers, colleagues and co-workers respect and listen to each other while also providing encouragement and constructive feedback. Senior management has a particular responsibility for making resources available, managing opposition in the organisation and eliminating obstacles to innovation. It should not really be very difficult to set the stage for innovation, and yet it can often be tricky to put it into practice. It may sometimes seem easier to get people to toe the line by employing a carrot and stick approach and/or by mobilising the group, the company or even the nation to defend itself against an external enemy, because in the short term it can, unfortunately, be more effective to play on people's inner fears than to build on their strengths.

In recent years, market conditions have been completely transformed by radical technological innovations. The global transfer of knowledge and increasing international competition are redefining the playing field for companies and organisations. A new company can be set up very quickly, while existing companies need to act in a completely different way if they are to survive in the long run. With the fourth industrial revolution underway, it is clear that everything is simply going to move faster and faster. There will be ever-increasing demands for innovation and development, and we are only just seeing the start of it.

Both researchers and journalists like to present Google as one of today's most successful and innovative businesses, having introduced numerous innovations of both a radical and an incremental nature. Google is certainly an amazing inspiration, but Google's world is not one that is shared by other companies and so it cannot simply be copied. As one of the most sought-after employers in the world, they can choose to recruit only those people who have the best possible skills and expressly share the company's values.

That would probably be a utopia for most companies and organisations. The reality is different for those organisations that are not working at the cutting edge of technology or communications or constantly creating new markets. Most of them operate within, and supply, our traditional existing markets and have co-workers who are quite ordinary people.

Does that mean that businesses of this sort cannot innovate both radically and incrementally and achieve success? Of course not, but to do so they must start from the position in which the organisation finds itself and make the most of the energy and knowledge they already have. The best way to do this is to work consistently towards an attractive corporate culture with a positive work climate and good leadership whilst at the same time allowing space for the organisation's intrapreneurs to step forward.

One step that is quite commonly taken these days is to establish an accelerator or an incubator for innovation. This involves starting up new processes or physical companies/subsidiaries in which the company's intrapreneurs are given opportunities similar to those they would have if they were entrepreneurs in their own business. One advantage of an incubator is that the finances, staff and other resources can be kept separate from the regular business activity. The intrapreneurs get space for ideas and innovation while the regular operations are spared some of the disruption that always comes with intrapreneurship and innovation.

The incubator solution is not entirely positive. Those working on innovation can easily become isolated from everyday events and thus from reality. That can happen if the intrapreneur has no natural link to the organisation's regular business and does not encounter the day-to-day challenges and problems that can trigger creativity and generate ideas. At the same time, it can be difficult for intrapreneurs themselves to identify the right people from amongst a large workforce and to link their cross-cutting skills to the intrapreneurial team in the incubator. That could make them dependent on management supplying these resources, thus limiting the extent to which they have control over both the process and the skills. It is also important to manage internal opposition to change when subsequently attempting to introduce an innovation into an existing organisation.

It is essential that the intrapreneurs are involved in the company's day-to-day activity and are able to build their own personal network of colleagues and co-workers and of internal and external customers. For an intrapreneur, being challenged and encountering opposition while having their endurance put to the test is not purely negative. The experience may act as a spur that welds the intrapreneurial team together more quickly and keeps them more on their toes. Obviously, the aim is for the work climate generally to be positive and pleasant, but it does not harm intrapreneurs to encounter the day-to-day realities. In fact, the opposite is true; if done in the right way, it will strengthen them as individuals and also enhance the company's collective ability to innovate.

Those at the top of companies and organisations face a major challenge firstly in identifying and then understanding the needs of their own intrapreneurs and then finding ways to meet those needs. Theirs is a balancing act that requires mastering the art of giving intrapreneurs the right amount of freedom and allowing them to be successful while at the same time managing, developing and maintaining their interaction with the organisation's functioning day-to-day operations.

My conclusion is that there is everything to be gained from finding ways to make the interaction work. What is important is creating an environment that gives people space and resources and supports development and innovation. First and foremost, we need courageous owners, boards, managers and management teams that share a vision about what real development means for their organisation and that stand up for that vision.

Leaders who accept the challenge of leading an organisation that is in a state of constant change.

With increased knowledge and awareness, individuals will feel more secure in themselves and thus more creative and innovative, while there will also be greater understanding and tolerance of differences. This in turn means people will become better at working collaboratively. Once more and more co-workers understand these connections, the company can *stop looking for miracle workers* – because they will already have them in their organisation.

A supplementary question: What happens to intrapreneurs when all the opposition and hard work is behind them and the goal has been achieved? What happens when the impossible has become the possible, so that this then becomes the norm for the organisation and both management and co-workers view their new situation as the baseline position? When a new truth has been created to replace the old one? How does an intrapreneur find inspiration, energy and the strength to continue developing? This is where management has a significant responsibility in choosing a strategy that boosts intrapreneurs' intrinsic motivation, as it is management that must show the way and identify what is important. The strategy must include both how to lead intrapreneurs – genuinely positive people who may be unaware of their intrapreneurial nature – to success, and how to help create an environment that suits all co-workers.

If everything goes well, an intrapreneur can bring in new thinking and ideas, inspiration, visions, job satisfaction, problem-solving, resilience, courage and, in many cases, achieve quite extraordinary results. Once you have read this book you will know a little more than most people about how intrapreneurs work, and about attitudes and situations that can promote, or work against, innovation. This will give you the opportunity, and the challenge, of making the most of the intrapreneurs in your organisation and of starting to lead development instead of simply going along with it.

I hope that, as an owner, board member or CEO, you will feel inspired and motivated to invest even more in your organisation's collective ability to innovate. If you are a manager, a colleague or a co-worker of an intrapreneur, I hope you will feel better equipped to manage any differences between you. For those of you who are intrapreneurs, meanwhile, I hope that you will have gained a greater understanding of yourself and of other people and can see how you can use that knowledge in a positive way to continue driving innovation.

The opportunity is now yours to come together to create an improved work environment with good management, employeeship and successful innovation

A guide for leaders, managers and intrapreneurs

To round off the book, I share my experiences of intrapreneurship, and those of other people, in the form of a guide that includes practical advice and recommendations for anyone managing intrapreneurship and innovation as part of their day-to-day work. It is aimed mainly at leaders, managers and intrapreneurs, but it may be useful to anyone affected in some way by intrapreneurship in the workplace. The object is to facilitate communication and create a sound basis for a successful working relationship at an early stage.

The first section comprises my recommendations to senior management in companies and organisations about what an employer needs to think about when planning to take on an intrapreneur. Following that, there are some suggested actions for those wanting to know how to get the most out of the intrapreneurs already employed with them. Finally, I provide some practical advice to those with an intrapreneurial personality and who are either seeking employment as a change leader or are already active as intrapreneurs within an organisation. Some intrapreneurs may find the advice challenging and difficult to act on. To a certain extent, it is based on approaches and behaviours that do not come naturally to people with an intrapreneurial personality. It may feel uncomfortable to have to concern yourself with detail, consider potential obstacles and risks and to ask, or be asked, difficult questions when what you actually want to do is discuss challenges and opportunities. In a recruitment situation this might feel negative and detract from any pleasure or positive feelings about the assignment, both for the intrapreneur and the prospective employer. But if this is approached the right way, the change project should be able to get off to a flying start.

Recommendations to senior management/employers:

– if you are planning to employ, or have already taken on, an intrapreneur or change leader

Employing a change leader or intrapreneur is often expensive, partly because the person appointed may command a high salary but mainly because change projects in themselves come at a high price. They cost money and divert time, energy and resources from day-to-day work. Of course, the greatest cost comes as the result of a change project that fails. The risk of failure is highest if an organisation recruits an external change leader without fully analysing its own needs and the consequences of appointing someone in that role.

Do your homework before starting the project

It is important for management to have a credible *innovation strategy* to support recruitment for a change project. Before embarking on a recruitment process, the company should have a discussion about what it wants from the person it employs and the price it is prepared to pay for bringing in and retaining the unique skills that an intrapreneur has. It must analyse and assess the consequences as, with their different motivating factors, needs and behaviours, an intrapreneur will undoubtedly "disrupt" the company's existing work.

Ask questions both of individuals and of management collectively, e.g.:
- What type of change and innovation is needed in the organisation in respect of the outside world and what will its scope be?
- How will the organisation's existing work be affected?
- Are funding and resources available, or will projects compete with the normal business operation?
- Has management got the interest, authority, courage and strength to drive the change in the face of the internal opposition that is certain to arise as part of the process?
- Are the members of the management team fully aware of what drives them, their approach to risk and their attitude to procedures and rules?

- Do they trust and have confidence in each other when the team is faced with making difficult decisions?

' Who in the organisation and in the management team is best suited to act as the sponsor/protector of the intrapreneur?

Put plans in place to "protect" the intrapreneur

In any innovation process, it is not the intrapreneur's responsibility to adjust to the existing organisation. For the process to be successful, the management team must have an understanding of the type of personality the intrapreneur has. In other words, they must understand, accept and have the courage to address the intrapreneur's visions and motivations, need for inspiration and new knowledge, and need to work together with others in cross-functional teams. It is essential for management to take steps to protect the intrapreneur within the organisation from political power-play, risk aversion, rigid rules and procedures and having to compete for resources.

Communicate the company's vision and values

It is important that management is able to successfully communicate a clear vision and the values that underpin the organisation as a whole, along with a view of the way forward and how the individual project connects with it. The attitude and behaviour of the management team will be crucial in terms of how important other managers and co-workers consider the project to be, and will thus determine whether the organisation supports or scuppers the intrapreneur's ongoing work.

Share information and knowledge about the projects

For a project to be successful, the management team needs to share its thinking both about the innovation strategy as a whole and about the individual project. Information should be made available to all managers and all the intrapreneur's prospective colleagues and co-workers; the more involved they are from the outset, the easier it will be to implement the changes. Doing this will also help middle managers, colleagues and co-workers understand and accept intrapreneurial projects and any "exemptions" that might otherwise be perceived as benefits.

Do not accept risk aversion or any other restrictive behaviour

Management needs to make it clear that any undermining of the intrapreneur's task is unacceptable. If a manager or co-worker nonetheless does attempt to obstruct the intrapreneur's work, it is important that management listens to both parties and openly distances itself from restrictive or negative behaviour in both its words and its actions.

Provide support for the necessary administration and planning

Since procedures and rules can kill off an intrapreneur's motivation and inspiration, the responsibility for complying with them in practice should not be given to the intrapreneur. This is important because the organisation should do its best to avoid the intrapreneur seeming "negligent and not very professional" or being perceived by colleagues and co-workers as having VIP privileges – something that may happen if they take a different approach to prioritisation. So the responsibility for monitoring any rules and procedures that are particularly important and necessary for the company's day-to-day operations should be given to someone else. Ideally, this person would be a co-worker who is part of the intrapreneurial team and trusted by the intrapreneur.

Do not underestimate the start-up phase

In some ways, an intrapreneur who has been working in secret on new projects in the workplace is more likely to be successful than someone recruited directly as a change leader. Expectations and time pressure are a major factor here. A person employed with the explicit expectation that they will make successful changes – that will ideally quickly turn a profit – may find it difficult to secure enough lead-in time before the demand for measurable results starts to affect their work. As the intrapreneur's strength is in their holistic approach and their connection with the organisation's vision and values, it is very important that they are given time to gather and collate all essential information and any data needed to inform their decisions. Once that job is complete, the rest of the work tends to be done relatively quickly, but the quality of the project is determined by how well the initial groundwork is done. An intrapreneur who operates unnoticed "under the radar" can do this initial piece of work without the time pressure that goes with it.

Plan actions that will inspire and motivate your intrapreneur

Intrapreneurs move quickly from ideas to action, and they listen and process the thoughts and ideas of those around them. So they need access to skilled colleagues and external experts so that they can test the validity of their own thinking as various alternatives emerge. An intrapreneur will often need to get themselves a grounding in a variety of different areas. They will see this as essential in helping them to get an understanding, and create an overall picture, of where the project is going and what needs to be done. It may, at the same time, be difficult for them to articulate the exact purpose of the various initiatives, as they will be acting on their gut feelings. The employer will be wise to support these initiatives without too much questioning. A budget should be set aside from the start to cover these kinds of extra cost.

Enhance the expertise of the management team and the board

Make sure that there is at least one person in management with the knowledge, interest and experience needed to assess the strategic innovations proposed by the intrapreneur. If management does not have the right skills or is unaware of, or unconcerned about, their own lack of knowledge, the project will fail. There will naturally be a greater degree of risk aversion in situations where management does not feel it has a good command of a particular area. Where that is the case, it is very unlikely that management will see or be able to take advantage of the opportunities presented by the intrapreneur's vision and project. If management is aware of its limitations, it can choose to actively seek out expertise, perhaps using external resources to aid its decision-making.

Reward middle managers who actively support the intrapreneur

An operational manager is normally judged on the basis of factors such as productivity, efficiency, profitability, and satisfied customers and co-workers. Their role is to help establish and maintain a flexible and well-functioning workplace that is largely free of conflict and disruption. A change project will normally disrupt most of the above, since the aim of development and change is, to some extent, to turn what is already in place upside down. The changes will themselves have an impact on existing processes and procedures, making co-workers feel less secure. Because of this, it is important that management supports and educates any operational managers involved and acknowledges and rewards those middle managers who are able to operate "ambidextrously", i.e. those who can manage day-to-day operations while also supporting their intrapreneurs and their change projects.

Advice to intrapreneurs

Some of the advice to intrapreneurs might be seen as inhibiting the energy in the room when a manager and an intrapreneur meet, which makes it less likely that they will choose to talk about difficult issues.

So it is helpful if the member of HR staff or recruiter in charge is aware of how important these issues are for ensuring successful work on change. As professionals, they can support both parties and make sure that they take time to run through the issues properly.

If you are seeking employment as a change leader:

Ask questions and try not to be try not to be too starry-eyed.

Actively researching the organisation and asking questions will give you a realistic picture of what you can expect at your prospective workplace. You might have questions about the organisation's structure, culture, work climate, management, technical level, administration, allocation of resources, politics, view on risk-taking or rules and regulations. It is important to ask questions *before* you accept an offer of employment, even if you feel enthused and challenged by the proposed new tasks and just want to focus on all the opportunities. Be sure to ask even if you find some of the issues difficult to raise. If you do not feel you have the clear support of HR or a recruiter, it is a good idea to use a checklist and to practice before the interview so that you do not leave out any important questions.

Get acquainted with the organisation's vision and values

As an intrapreneur, it is crucial that you believe in your project, but it is just as important that you believe in the overall benefit of the development you will be expected to lead. Ask yourself some general questions:
- Do you feel that you could be committed to the services or products the company or organisation provides to its customers?
- Are co-workers treated well by management?
- Is there a good atmosphere at the workplace?
- Do you agree with the anticipated benefit of the planned projects that you are expected to develop?

Your gut instinct is important here in deciding whether or not to accept the work.

Negotiate before you accept the role
Acquiring a picture for yourself of the organisation and its activities puts you in an excellent position to negotiate on the scope of the work, autonomy, responsibility, authority and access to resources. Make sure you negotiate before you are appointed, and do not be afraid to make your requirements clear. Both you and your prospective employer will benefit from having a realistic picture of what needs to happen to enable you to achieve the results requested.

Make sure your sponsor is able to protect you
As an intrapreneur, you need a sponsor/protector with enough power and influence to smooth your path, handle internal opposition and allocate resources. To be able to provide the necessary support, the sponsor themselves must be firmly established in the management team and the organisation, share your vision and have an understanding of the practical requirements of the business. The fact that someone has an important title does not necessarily mean that they have the ability or status to be your sponsor in practice. Make sure that you get to meet the person in question and try to ask more in-depth questions about what they might do if and when obstacles and conflict arise around aspects such as prioritisation, the timetable and resources. Consider their responses and whether it seems likely that this sponsor/protector is the right person for the role. The sponsor/protector is the key to your success!

Guard against unrealistic expectations and timescales
It takes time both to identify areas that need change and to implement change. Because the management team is under constant pressure to deliver planned results, they may have unrealistic expectations as to the amount of time the work on change may or can be allowed to take. Have a frank discussion about management's expectations in respect of the timetable and see how they react to uncertainty around the length of the project and the estimated costs/resource needs.

Safeguard your personal energy – keep your own batteries charged

Intrapreneurs are characterised by their unselfishness and total commitment, qualities that often lead them to make personal sacrifices to achieve the results that are important to them. This can lead to a situation in which you are constantly giving, and this can sap your energy if you are not able, or do not take the time, to do things that stimulate you and build up your inner strength. What you choose to do is up to you, but it is important to do something, even if it means temporarily focusing on something other than your work. Tell your prospective employer if you have any specific needs, e.g. flexible working hours, personal development or training, access to external contacts and networks or any special equipment.

If you are already working as an intrapreneur or change leader:

Replenish your sources of creativity

As an intrapreneur, your need to use your own creativity and learn interesting things by being challenged in your work is so important that this in itself can determine whether or not you will stay with a particular employer. Be aware of this and tell your employer of your need for training in current areas of activity and potentially also in new ones, access to cross-functional skills, external contacts and networks, etc. Make sure your employer understands this, and confirm to them that, for you, this is one of the linchpins of successful innovation.

Avoid becoming the organisation's "change guru"

It is easy for intrapreneurs to take on too much responsibility in a wider context and to become the person presented as being responsible for all innovation in the company or organisation. That can be flattering but also very lonely. The management team may choose to "buy itself out" by referring to you as the person dealing with change in the organisation. If that happens, it is particularly important that you have previously ensured that you have the right to make decisions about and control the resources you need.

By all means work "under the radar", but only with the support of a sponsor

It is neither unusual nor inappropriate for an intrapreneur to work on a project in secret during its initial stages. Sometimes it is absolutely essential, because internal opposition and critics would otherwise kill off the project before it has got off the ground. Whether or not that is an appropriate strategy depends entirely on how ready the organisation is for change. As an intrapreneur, you need a sponsor/protector if you are to be able to make your vision a reality and also to sell your vision to management and get more resources. If you cannot find a sponsor at your workplace, you are in the wrong place.

Make sure you get "slack resources" to develop your ideas

Even if you are not the sort of person that makes plans, it is important to deliberately create some blank space in your diary every week. You need to set aside some time for yourself so that you can reflect on various ideas, options and opportunities and find fresh inspiration. If every working day is fully booked with meetings and daily tasks, you will be limited as to how far you can be creative and satisfy your curiosity. It is important for the project that you give yourself time to achieve some perspective and to reflect, at the same time as it is crucial for your intrinsic motivation that your work feels meaningful and that you are able to develop as an individual.

The Intrapreneur's Ten Commandments – a checklist

Gifford Pinchot III (1985) has drawn up what he refers to as his "Ten Commandments" for an intrapreneur:

1. Come to work each day willing to be fired.

2. Circumvent any orders aimed at stopping your dream.

3. Do any job needed to make your project work, regardless of your job description.

4. Find people to help you.

5. Follow your intuition about the people you choose and work only with the best.

6. Work underground as long as you can, publicity triggers the corporate immune system.

7. Never bet on a race unless you are running in it.

8. Remember, it is easier to ask forgiveness than for permission.

9. Be true to your goals but be realistic about the ways to achieve them.

10. Honor your sponsors.

Acknowledgements

This book is based on a wide range of research and the personal and professional experiences of many people. I would like to express my sincere gratitude to all the employees and intrapreneurs who have shared their stories with me and provided me with new insights, thereby making this book possible.

My thanks go to all the researchers, prominent and less prominent, who have written and documented their studies and made them available to the rest of us. It has been a pleasure to have access to their in-depth knowledge in a number of areas enabling me, in true intrapreneurial spirit, to merge many different ideas, skills and experiences into a new whole.

My family has been very supportive throughout and I thank my sons, Thomas and Magnus, as well as Vanessa, Oscar, Malidza and Lisa and family, for their understanding and patience during the years when I have focused solely on writing. A special thank-you to my parents, Ulla and Torsten , for their generous support.

My colleague Ewa Granath has been a source of calm energy and encouragement, reading and commenting on the manuscript several times and providing valuable feedback.

Editor Katarina Vastamäki worked on the structure and editing of the original (Swedish) book and gave me much good advice along the way.

Edwina Simpson has done a great job translating the book into English, while maintaining the tone and spirit of the original. I am very grateful to all three of them.

I dedicate this book to my dear partner and supporter, Per-Olof Larsson, whose broad skills and experience enabled him to contribute ideas and creative thinking, while being invaluable as my sounding board and coach.

About the author

Even when I started working on this book about intrapreneurs and innovation I was wondering what it was that was making me do it. After several years spent reviewing the research, undertaking interviews and writing, I conclude that this is once again an example of my drive to develop and change and my desire to do things differently. It is evidence that I am motivated by understanding connections, learning new things and finding new solutions, because I am an intrapreneur who always sees opportunities and wants to change things that do not work.

My need to explore innovation and intrapreneurship in more depth arises from a long-held desire for an explanation as to why it is that several of my innovatory projects have gone extremely well while others have been much less successful. On analysing the various projects, it became clear that the circumstances were different in each case, but it was nevertheless difficult to put into words both what the differences were and how significant they were in terms of the end result. So I wanted to find out whether we could have done things differently.

In hindsight, I can say with some certainty that the latter projects lacked several of the factors that are essential to successful innovation. With the knowledge I now have, based on research and other people's experiences, I am convinced that we could have avoided a number of classic errors and that our outcomes could have been completely different and much more positive.

By way of background: just like many other intrapreneurs, I was aware at an early stage that I was a bit different from the people around me. It was noticeable when I started working that I saw things differently to many of my then managers, colleagues and co-workers, but I did not really understand what the differences were. It was not until I was working as a consultant that I had sufficient perspective to be able to think more deeply about what it was that marked my years as an employee, twenty of which were spent in the role of manager and change leader.

Throughout my career, my need for development and change has been a consistent and significant feature. After university, I started work as an accountant, but there were other things that interested me more than accountancy. So I set up and ran my own business for a few years before accepting the post of CFO at a company that was part of a major group.

Over the following years, I held a range of positions including product manager, marketing director and head of sales. I was then involved in a start-up for a couple of years and worked as a finance and management consultant. These days I am also a writer focusing on intrapreneurship and innovation.

What my many different roles and commissions have in common is that there is a logical progression to them, or so it seems to me now in retrospect. Each new position arose from my need to learn more and to have opportunities to develop various projects further. So as soon as I felt restricted in my existing role, I looked for a new position where I would have more opportunity to achieve results. During my almost fifteen years as an employee in one company, I had six different roles in which I was constantly working to develop and change the company's services, products, processes, systems, marketing and sales.

Many, but not all, of the innovatory projects were a great success. Having examined the research and interviewed some intrapreneurs, I now feel able to propose a description of the projects that were most successful. If you have read the book, you will recognise Fredrickson's positivity factors, Ekvall's creativity factors for an innovative work climate, Amabile et al's theories about intrinsic motivation and Pinchot's description of intrapreneurship when they appear in my analysis below:

"In our most successful projects, I (the intrapreneur) and my co-workers (the intrapreneurial team) were interested in and inspired by our task. The members of the group respected each other's expertise and ideas, and trusted and had confidence in one another. We had a great deal of freedom in our work, were certain that what we were doing was important and were optimistic about our chances of success. We all believed that we could achieve our very ambitious goals and were not afraid of failure.

Our manager was interested, encouraging and offered time and resources. We learned new things, enjoyed each other's company, got pleasure from our task and had fun working together. Once we had achieved our goal, we felt a sense of pride and celebrated with the rest of the company before we moved on to our next challenge.

Some of our colleagues and other co-workers felt that what we were doing was unnecessary and that we worked in an unstructured way, sometimes in a state of chaos. We often encountered significant internal resistance to change, and at times had to work under the radar so that our project was not halted at an early stage. I had to be very stubborn and spend a lot of time patiently explaining and selling the project to the management team. I was often successful in this, but not always.

The successful projects helped the company to:
' Launch both new and redeveloped products and services
' Build strong brands
' Win national and international awards and prizes
' Attract new customers
' Generate significant financial profit

Once we had been successful with the first projects, management started to accept us more and it was easier to get support for the next project."

I am now convinced that it is possible to learn how to drive successful innovation in companies and organisations by sharing other people's knowledge and experience and using employees' talents in the right way. What is required is hard work, a strong will and an awareness of the need to earn other people's respect, trust and confidence, because we can only create innovation by working together with others. I hope that this book will help make your journey towards innovation a little easier.

Birgitte Stjärne

Summary

What follows is a summary of a selection of the concepts and research theories discussed in the various sections. I have not, however, referenced the interviews with intrapreneurs and the analysis and conclusions relating to them.

Chapter 1 – About intrapreneurs and intrapreneurship

' New competitors constantly challenge by renewing products and services or developing brand new ones. The changes are often disruptive, radical and alter the very premises on which the organisation is based. So a capacity for continuous innovation is a key competency (Steiber).

' Intrapreneurs are employees who are both visionaries and implementers of change mainly in large companies and organisations. The term "intrapreneur" is an abbreviation of "intra-corporate entrepreneur" (Pinchot).

' Employees who drive innovation have been called different things; they may be known as "innovators", "intrapreneurs" or "internal entrepreneurs". "Intrapreneur" is the only one of these that is used in one distinct way and so is the term used in this book.

' Researchers and industry agree that an organisation's co-workers are the most important factor in successful innovation. The challenge for companies is to attract talented individuals who want autonomous, creative and meaningful tasks. At the same time, many organisations fail to change their structures and management so that they can develop and retain their intrapreneurs

' Putting an intrapreneur's ideas into practice requires resources such as capital, access to production and marketing resources, expertise and cross-functional skills. This means that management, human resources and the work environment are crucial to an intrapreneur's success.

' Intrapreneurs are often compared with entrepreneurs. Entrepreneurs are self-employed people who have control of their own business and who take considerable personal and financial risks. Intrapreneurs work in established organisations, take less financial risk and have greater access to resources, but often encounter strong resistance and internal barriers.

' Intrapreneurs establish cross-functional intrapreneurial teams with a broad range of skills. The intrapreneur and the team need support from a "sponsor", perhaps an owner, a CEO or previous intrapreneur, or a "protector", someone in top management (Pinchot).

' Intrapreneurs are driven mainly by intrinsic motivation and have specific qualities and motivating factors. They are driven by an opportunity to combine their own vision with that of the organisation, seek out challenges and find solutions to problems. They like to work autonomously and are constantly seeking personal development.

Chapter 2 – Influencing the ability to innovate

' "Innovation" as a concept is normally divided into incremental, stepwise innovation and radical, disruptive innovation (Schumpeter).

' Incremental innovations
  - are small changes that gradually reinforce previous knowledge
  - simplify functions, but do not change human behaviour and are not groundbreaking

' Radical innovations
  - generate fundamental changes in functions, activity and behaviours
  - are creative, disruptive changes that break down and/or replace existing structures

' The type of creative acts/innovations that take place in an organisation can be determined by the work climate (Ekvall).

- In Ekvall's view, certain factors are essential for a creative work climate. Co-workers need:
    - Challenge, involvement and autonomy
    - Workplace relationships that are based on trust and openness
    - Time to reflect and monitor
    - To have fun at work, whilst always having plenty to hold their attention
    - An atmosphere of open debate and a lack of conflict
    - To feel that they are allowed to take risks and make mistakes

- The degree of freedom, liveliness, debate, dialogue and risk-taking in a work climate determines whether it will support radical or incremental innovation.

- Personal motivation can be divided into extrinsic and intrinsic motivation (Deci & Ryan). Individuals are driven by intrinsic or extrinsic motivation, and sometimes by both.

- Intrinsic motivation
    - arises spontaneously and cannot be forced
    - builds on internal stimuli, such as personal interest, pleasure or a sense of meaningfulness
    - leads to a tendency to act intrapreneurially – makes it easier to learn new things, assimilate ideas and deal with set-backs and problems

- Extrinsic motivation is based on external stimuli, which could be a good reputation, status or financial reward.

- It is common for both top management and managers at other levels in companies and organisations to unwittingly undermine their co-workers' intrinsic motivation through their negative attitudes (Amabile & Kramer).

- There are parallels between credible leadership (Kouzes & Posner) and intrapreneurship. Just like intrapreneurs, successful leaders:
  - Adhere to their own values and affirm shared values
  - Inspire a shared vision and see opportunities
  - Challenge processes and initiate innovative ways of improving them
  - Allow failure
  - Promote cooperation by building trust
  - Strengthen others by enhancing their self-determination and skills
  - Acknowledge co-workers' achievements, whether major or minor, and show appreciation of their unique skills

Chapter 3 - Factors influencing the intrapreneur and the work environment

- Research on positive psychology shows that positive emotional experiences help us to become more open and accepting, making us more creative and more optimistic (Fredrickson).

- The positive emotions come out of how we think, i.e. how we interpret events, experiences, thoughts and ideas. Those who experience more positive emotions can cope better with set-backs and stress.

- Teams whose members act creatively and supportively and who talk to each other in an encouraging, helpful and approving way achieve much greater profitability and customer satisfaction (Losada).

- Unique to human beings is the prefrontal cortex, the front part of the brain that gives us our ability to think, process information, make decisions and feel empathy. It is likely that feelings of motivation arise from activity in these groups of nerve cells.

- Our thoughts, emotions and behaviours, and thus the basis of our personal qualities and attitudes/habits, are all formed in our brain. The front parts of the brain are highly active when we are learning new, complex behaviours, but as things become habitual activity in this area declines.

- Willpower is an inner strength that enables us to control ourselves and resist short-term satisfaction so that we can achieve more long-term goals. It requires patience and commitment. The more mental exertion a task requires, the harder it becomes to take on the next big challenge, and this makes great demands on our willpower (Baumeister, Inzlicht et al).

- Patience is an attitude; it is the ability to wait without losing interest, perseverance, endurance and being able to accept disappointment. Most long-term goals and innovations require patience as there are sure to be errors and mistakes on the road to the optimum solution.

- Our conscious and unconscious choices of approach and attitude govern our behaviour and how we view and communicate with other people. We all react to change differently depending on what drives us and our basic approach to life.

Chapter 4 – Barriers to intrapreneurship

- There may be obstacles to intrapreneurship and innovation at different levels in the organisation, from the highest strategic levels – owners, board members and CEOs – to other managers, colleagues and co-workers.

- Conflicts of interest between intrapreneurs, colleagues and co-workers can create opposition and barriers between those who are in favour of major changes in the organisation and those who are against.

- Barriers may arise because innovation is not on the management team's agenda and is not discussed regularly. Management's focus is on day-to-day matters, short-term goals and operational issues (Kalling).

- There is no-one in the management team who can act as a sponsor or protector of the intrapreneur (Pinchot).

- Other barriers may include limited financial resources, geographical distance or co-workers lacking slack resources to develop their ideas (Kalling).

- A management team that takes a short-term view of profitability and efficiency and/or is opposed to risk-taking limits opportunities for innovation. It can mean that a company invests in mature technologies and in solutions that are similar to already tried-and-tested ones because they are afraid of taking risks (Ahuja & Lampert).

- One major barrier can be a lack of reward and recognition for success combined with negative consequences in the event of failure (Ahuja & Lampert).

- Difficulties may arise when intrapreneurs and entrepreneurs work together. Entrepreneurs may put their efforts into their own ideas/innovations, and are stubborn, driven people who put their ideas into practice and are used to making the decisions. By contrast, intrapreneurs focus on the big picture, are driven by development and opportunities and are often used to having access to resources. They need freedom and have little regard for authority.

Chapter 5 – The means to achieving successful intrapreneurship

- Researchers say that the ability to be continuously innovative is a critical business skill for most companies today, irrespective of sector, and a strategic responsibility for the board and senior management (Steiber & Alänge).

- The theme for the 2016 World Economic Forum was "The Fourth Industrial Revolution" In 2020, a combination of billions of people with smartphones and new technological breakthroughs in areas such as artificial intelligence, robotics, the Internet of Things, autonomous vehicles etc. will create a whole new set of realities for companies globally (Schwab).

- The employees of the future will need to adapt their knowledge and capabilities to keep up with demand. In 2020, creativity is expected to rank third amongst the capabilities required by employers, rising from tenth in 2015 (report from the World Economic Forum).

- Google's management model includes corporate culture, leadership, organisational structure and value and reward systems as important parameters for innovation (Steiber).

- Companies focus too much on control and quality rather than on knowledge of how to create and develop value-adding innovative strategies and renewed business systems and models (Steiber).

- Management should identify an overall direction for the organisation. By creating opportunities for experimentation and building up expertise, managers can help boost the motivation of their co-workers, not least by offering challenges and stimulating tasks.

- The employees that are most in demand in successful Silicon Valley companies have the same characteristics as intrapreneurs.

- The best co-workers (Steiber & Alänge) are:
    - Entrepreneurial by nature and passionate about their work
    - Constantly questioning the current state of play and the status quo
    - Individualistic, strong-minded, collaborative and adaptable all at once
    - Striving for personal satisfaction, but are also very committed team players who want to be part of something bigger
    - Clever, enquiring and humble

- The same successful companies are still led today by the innovative entrepreneurs that started them. The founders retain their original values and take a long-term approach to leadership (Steiber).

References

The researchers and authors cited in this book are presented here in alphabetical order and then in the form of references.

Aertsen, Ad Professor of Neurobiology and Biophysics Director, Bernstein Center, Freiburg, Germany

Ahuja, Gautam Professor of Business Administration, Professor of Strategy, University of Michigan Ross, USA

Alänge, Sverker Associate professor Technology Management and Economics, Chalmers Tekniska Högskola, Göteborg, Sweden

Amabile, Theresa M. Edsel Bryant Ford Professor of Business Administration at Harvard Business School, Harvard University, Boston, USA

Amorós, José Ernesto Professor, School of Economics and Business, Universidad del Desarrollo, Chile

Antončič, Boštjan Professor of Entrepreneurship, University of Ljubljana, Slovenia

Bahuguna, Jyotika Ph.D. Computational Neuroscience, Postdoctoral Researcher, Juelich Forshungszentrum, Germany

Baruah, Bidyut Associate lecturer in Engineering Education and Management Research Group, Department of Electronics, University of York, United Kingdom

Baumeister, Roy F. Francis Eppes Eminent Scholar and Professor of Psychology, Florida State University, USA

Bosma, Niels Assistant Professor Utrecht University School of Economics and Research fellow vid Vlerick Business School, the Netherlands

Calakos, Nicole M.D., Ph.D., Associate Professor of Neurology and Neurobiology, Duke University Medical Center, Durham, North Carolina, USA

Chrisman, James J. Professor of Management, Mississippi State University, USA

Crick, Francis (1916–2004) British molecular biologist, biophysics and brain researcher, Nobel Prize winner 1962 in the "Nobel Prize in Physiology or Medicine", Distinguished Research Professor Salk Institute for Biological Studies, La Jolla, California, USA

de Jong, Jeroen Professor in Marketing and Business Development, Utrecht University School of Economics, the Netherlands

Deci, Edward L. Professor of Psychology and Gowen Professor in the Social Sciences, University of Rochester, USA

Denti, Leif	Ph.D. at the Department of Psychology, Göteborgs Universitet, Sweden
Ekvall, Göran	(1930-2012) Professor emeritus in organisational psychology, Lunds universitet, Sweden
Engberg, Isabel	Student/author of a Master's thesis 2014, Department of Social Sciences, Södertörns högskola, Stockholm, Sweden
Ericsson, Anders	Swedish psychologist and Conradi Eminent Scholar, Professor of Psychology, Florida State University, USA
Feldman Barrett, Lisa	Distinguished Professor of Psychology, Northeastern University, Canada
Francis, Zoë	Master of Arts, Psychology, University of Toronto, Canada
Fredrickson, Barbara	Professor of Psychology (the Kenan Distinguished Professor of Psychology), University of North Carolina, Chapel Hill, USA
Gagné, Marylene	Ph.D. Rochester University, Professor Management and Organisations, UWA Business School, University of Australia, Australia
Gailliot, Matthew	Ph.D. in Social Psychology, Florida State University, USA
Gartner, William B.	Professor of Entrepreneurship, California Lutheran University, USA and Copenhagen Business School, Denmark
Gladwell, Malcolm	Journalist and author in sociology and popular-Psychology, Canada/United Kingdom
Glaser, Jack	Professor of Psychology, University of California, Berkeley, USA
Gospic, Katarina	M.D., Ph.D. and a M.Sc. in Physiology, Cognitive Neuroscience, Karolinska Institutet, Stockholm, Sweden
Graybiel, Ann Martin	Investigator McGovern Institute, Professor, Department of Brain and Cognitive Sciences, Massachusetts Institute of Technology, USA
Heaphy, Emily	Assistant Professor of Organizational Behavior, Boston University, USA
Hennessey, Beth A.	Professor of Psychology, Wellesley College, Massachusetts, USA
Hisrich, Robert D.	Ph.D. Bridgestone Chair of International Marketing & Associate Dean of Graduate and International Programs, Kent State University, Cleveland, USA
Ingvar, Martin	Professor of Integrative Medicine at the Department of Clinical Neuroscience, Karolinska Institutet, Stockholm, Sweden
Inzlicht, Michel	Professor of Psychology, Toronto Laboratory for Social Neuroscience, University of Toronto, Canada

Janssen, Claes	Psychologist, researcher, author, teacher of pedagogy at Stockholm University, Associate Professor inOrganisation and Leadership at Socialhögskolan 1982–2007, Stockholm, Sweden
Kahneman, Daniel	Nobel Prize winner 2002 in the "Nobel Prize in Economics", Professor emeritus of Psychology, Princeton University, New Jersey, USA
Kalling, Thomas	Professor, Head of Business Administration, Lunds universitet, Lund, Sweden
Knowles, Eric D.	Associate Professor of Psychology, Department of Psychology, New York University, USA
Koch, Christof	President at the Allen Institute for Brain Science, Seattle,USA, former professor at California Institute of Technology, Pasadena, Kalifornien, USA
Kouzes, Jim	Dean's Executive Fellow of Leadership, Leavey School of Business Santa Clara University, California, USA
Kramer, Steven	Author and independent researcher, Ph.D. University of Virginia, USA
Krishnan, S. Shunmuga	System Software Engineer, senior, Akamai Technologies, Tirunelveli Area, India
Kumar, Arvind	Ph.D., Neuroscience, Cancer Research, Electrical Engineering, KTH, Kungliga Tekniska högskolan, Stockholm, Sweden
Lampert, Curba M.	Assistant Professor, Department of Management and International Business, Florida International University, USA
Losada, Macial	Psychologist, consultant, Ph.D. in organizational psychology, University of Michigan, USA
Lundström, Sara	Student/author of a Master's thesis 2014, Department of Social Sciences, Södertörns högskola, Stockholm, Sweden
Macrae, Neil C.	Professor Psychology, School of Psychology, University of Aberdeen, Aberdeen, United Kingdom
Maslow, Abraham	(1908–1970) Professor of Psychology at, among others, Brandeis University and Columbia University, USA
Mischel, Walter	Psychologist specialized in "personality theory and social psychology", Robert Johnston Niven Professor of Humane Letters in the Department of Psychology, New York, USA
Muraven, Mark	Professor of Psychology, University at Albany, State University of New York, USA

O'Hare, Justin	Researcher/graduate student in Neurobiology 2016, Duke University Medical Center, Durham, North Carolina, USA
Olson, Lars	Professor senior, Department of Neuroscience, Karolinska Institutet, Stockholm, Sweden
Parker, Simon C.	Professor of Entrepreneurship. Director, Entrepreneurship Cross-Enterprise Centre, Faculty Scholar, Western University, USA
Pellman, Ron	Engineer, author and former CEO at Pinchot & Company, Seattle, USA
Pinchot III, Gifford	Entrepreneur, author and one of the founders and CEO:s of the Pinchot University (former Bainbridge Graduate Institute), Seattle, USA
Posner, Barry	Professor of Leadership at the Leavey School of Business at Santa Clara University, California, USA
Pramodita, Sharma	Professor, Grossman School of Business, University of Vermont, USA
Ryan, Richard M.	Professor of Psychology, psychiatry and education, University of Rochester, New York, USA
Sapolsky, Robert	Professor of biology, Professor of Neurology and Neurological sciences, Stanford University, USA
Schmeichel, Brandon J.	Professor of Psychology, Texas A&M University, USA
Schumpeter, Joseph	(1883–1950) Austrian-German- American economist, professor at Harvard University, USA
Schwab, Klaus	Founder and Executive Chairman, World Economic Forum, Switzerland
Sinha, Nupur	Research Scholar, Department of Humanities and Social Sciences, Indian Institute of Technology, Kharagpur, India
Sitaraman, Ramesh K .	Professor, College of Information and Computer Sciences, University of Massachusetts, USA
Sokal, Alan	Professor of Mathematics at University College London, Professor of Physics at New York University, USA
Srivastava, Kailash B.L.	Ph.D. in Organizational Psychology, Positive Psychology, Quantitative Psychology, Indian Institute of Technology, Kharagpur, India

Stam, Erik	Professor and Head of Strategy, Organisation and Entrepreneurship at Utrecht University School of Economics, the Neatherlands
Stanovich, Keith E.	Professor emeritus, Applied Psychology and Human Development, University of Toronto, Canada
Steiber, Annika	Ph.D. in Management of Technology and Adjunct Professor, Santa Clara University, California, USA
Tierney, John	Journalist and author, New York Times, New York, USA
Tietz, Matthias	Assistant Professor of Entrepreneurship at IE Business School, Madrid, Spain
Tversky, Amos	(1937–1996) Psychologist, Ph.D. in cognitive psychology and behavioral economics, Stanford University, USA
Ward, Anthony	Professor in Engineering Management, Engineering Education and Management Research Group, University York, United Kingdom
Wennekers, Sander	Emeritus, Erasmus Center for Entrepreneurship research, Research Manager & Principal Investigator, Rotterdam School of Management, Erasmus University, the Netherlands
West, Richard F.	Professor emeritus, Department of Graduate
Zahra. Shaker A.	Psychology, James Madison University, USA Department chair, the Robert E. Buuck Chair of Entrepreneurship, Professor of strategy and Academic Director of the Gary S. Holmes Center for Entrepreneurship, the University of Minnesota, USA

References by chapter

Introduction

Steiber, A. (2014) expression "Kontinuerlig innovation en kärnkompetens" ("Continuous innovation, an essential core skill") retrieved from the report *Googlemodellen – Företagsledning för kontinuerlig innovation i en snabbföränderlig värld.,* Serie: VINNOVA Rapport VR 2014:03, ISBN 978-91-87537-12-7 Stiftelsen IMIT och VINNOVA

Kruege, A. (2015 May 18) article The rise of the intrapreneur. *Fast Company,* retrieved 20160925 from https://www.fastcompany.com/3046231/the-new-rules-of-work/the-rise-of-the-intrapreneur

Deloitte (2016) , *Millennials have one foot out the door, The Deloitte Millennial Survey 2016 ,* retrieved 20160925 from http://www2.deloitte.com/global/en/pages/about-deloitte/articles/gx-millennials-one-foot-out-the-door.html#loyal

Section 1 About intrapreneurs and intrapreneurship

Baruah B . & Ward A . (2014) Metamorphosis of intrapreneurship as an effective organizational strategy Researchgate.net. doi: 10.1007/s11365-014-0318-3, retrieved 20160620 from https://www.researchgate.net/profile/Tony_Ward8/publication/269222278_Metamorphosis_of_intrapreneurship_as_an_effective_organizational_strategy/links/54a4b2f60cf267bdb90679ef.pdf

What is intrapreneurship?

Macrae, N . "Pichot coined the term Intrapreneur", article 'Intrapreneurial Now: Big Goes Bust" . *The Economist* 7233.283: 47–52. (1982 April 17), retrieved 20161001 from https://www.intrapreneur.com/MainPages/History/Economist.html

Pinchot III, G. (1985). *Who is the Intrapreneur?* In: *Intrapreneuring: Why You Don't Have to Leave the Corporation to Become an Entrepreneur.* New York: Harper & Row

Zahra, S . A . (1995 Jan 1) Contextual influences on the corporate entrepreneurship - performance relationship: A longitudial analysis . *Journal of Business Venturing, 10* (1),. retrieved 20160501 from https://www.deepdyve.com/lp/elsevier/contextual-influences-on-the-corporate-entrepreneurship-performance-HjKll34800#

Antoncic, B . & Hisrich, R .D . (2003) Clarifying the intrapreneurship concept, Journal of Small Business and Enterprise Development, 10 (1), 7-24 . Doi 10.1108/14626000310461187, retrieved 20160201 from http://kisi.deu.edu.tr//ethem.duygulu/intrapreneurship%20antocic%20ve%20hisrich%202003.pdf

Gartner, W.B . (1988), Who is an entrepreneur? Is the wrong question. *Entrepreneurship Theory and Practice, 13*, 47-68, (1989). (Also interpreted by Bosma, Stam Wennekers 2012, p 2) , retrieved 20160202 from https://zabdesk.szabist.edu.pk/CoursePortFolioFiles/Mubin_1140_2758_1/who%20is%20an%20ent%20-%20lums.pdf

Gartner, W.B . (2005-06-07) interview and article by Jonas Gustafsson, *ESBRI*, Bill.Gartner, prisad professor och provokatör, retrieved 20160202 from http://www.esbri.se/artikel_visa.asp?id=334

Sharma, P . & Chrisman, J .J (1999) Toward a Reconciliation of the Definitional Issues in the Field of Corporate Entrepreneurship . Baylor University, retrieved 20160427 from http://www.cemi.com.au/sites/all/publications/Sharma%20and%20Chrisman%201999.pdf

Intrapreneurial structure and culture

Pinchot III, G. (1985). *Who is the Intrapreneur? In: Intrapreneuring: Why You Don't Have to Leave the Corporation to Become an Entrepreneur.* New York: Harper & Row .

What kind of people are intrapreneurs?

Pinchot III, G. (1985). *Who is the Intrapreneur? In: Intrapreneuring: Why You Don't Have to Leave the Corporation to Become an Entrepreneur.* New York: Harper & Row .

Pinchot III, G . (1987) . Innovation Through Intrapreneuring . *Research Management, XXX* (2). (1987 March–April*)*, retrieved 20160101 from http://www.utdallas.edu/~chasteen/Pinchot%20webpage%20on%20Intrapreneur.htm

Bosma, N., Wennekers, S. & Amorós, J. E. (2012). *The Global Entrepreneurship Monitor 2011 Extended report: entrepreneurs and entrepreneurial employees across the globe,* retrieved 20151101 from http://www.gemconsortium.org/report

What are the characteristics of an intrapreneur?

Pinchot III, G. (1985). *Who is the Intrapreneur? In: Intrapreneuring: Why You Don't Have to Leave the Corporation to Become an Entrepreneur.* New York: Harper & Row .

Jong, J.D. & Wennekers, S. (2008). *Intrapreneurship Conceptualizing entrepreneurial employee behavior,* Scientific Analysis of Entrepreneurship and SMEs (SCALES), Zoetermeer EIM, retrieved 20151201 from https://pdfs.semanticscholar.org/57b9/ad05109844d5a794ce6068b90ec2df840cd1.pdf

Independent intrapreneur or intrapreneur supported by management?

Bosma, N., Stam, E., & Wennekers, S. (2010). Intrapreneurship - an international study . Scientific Analysis of Entrepreneurship and SMEs (2010 Jan 12) . EIM Research Report Intrapreneurship_v9 .doc: Zoetermeer, retrieved 20151101 from
http://citeseerx.ist.psu.edu/viewdoc/download?doi=10.1.1.333.6885&rep=rep1&type=pdf

Karlsson Klas, cited from Engberg, I. & Lundström, S.(2014) *Att skapa en intraprenör – en studie om den organisatoriska kontextens betydelse för intraprenöriellt beteende* , a Master's thesis, Södertörns högskola, Department of Social Sciences, retrieved from www.diva-portal.se/smash/get/diva2:729972/FULLTEXT01.pdf, confirmed by Karlsson via email 20160925

Identifying intrapreneurs

Karlsson Klas, cited from Engberg, I. & Lundström, S.(2014) *Att skapa en intraprenör – en studie om den organisatoriska kontextens betydelse för intraprenöriellt beteende* , a Master's thesis, Södertörns högskola, Department of Social Sciences, retrieved from www.diva-portal.se/smash/get/diva2:729972/FULLTEXT01.pdf, confirmed by Karlsson via email 20160925

Being an intrapreneur or an entrepreneur

DN 2016 a debate article by Wallenberg. M., Wallenberg, J. & Wallenberg, P "Olyckligt för Sverige om unga entreprenörer flyttar" *Dagens Nyheter,*
DN. (20160614), retrieved 20160901 from http://www.dn.se/debatt/olyckligt-for-sverige-om-unga-entreprenorer-flyttar/

Parker Simon C . (2009) . Intrapreneurship or entrepreneurship? *Journal of Business Venturing 26* 19–34, (2011) , retrieved 20160505 from http://www.dge.ubi.pt/msilva/Papers_MECE/Paper_8.pdf

Tietz, M . A . & Parker, S . C . (2012) How do intrapreneurs and entrepreneurs differ in their motivation to start a new venture? *Frontiers of Entrepreneurship Research,* 32 (4), retrieved 20160505 from http://digitalknowledge.babson.edu/cgi/viewcontent.cgi?artic-le=2390&context=fer

Intrapreneurship and entrepreneurship within organisations

Reports – GEM Global Entrepreneurship Monitor (2015/2016), retrieved 20160505 from http://www.gemconsortium.org/report

Braunerhjelm, P., Holmquist, C., Nyström, K., Stuart Hamilton, U. & Thulin,P.(2012) *Entreprenörskap i Sverige, Nationell rapport 2012.* Stockholm: Entreprenörskapsforum and GEM , retrieved 20151201 from http://entreprenorskapsforum.se/wp-content/uploads/2012/06/GEM_Nationell_Rapport_2012_WEBB_.pdf

Bosma, N., Stam, E., & Wennekers, S. (2010). *Intrapreneurship—an international study.* Scientific Analysis of Entrepreneurship and SMEs, EIM Research Report Intrapreneurship_v9.doc. Zoetermeer, (2010 Jan 12). , retrieved 20151101 from http://citeseerx.ist.psu.edu/viewdoc/download?doi=10.1.1.333.6885&rep=rep1&type=pdf

Bosma, N., Stam, E., & Wennekers, S. (2011) *Intrapreneurship Versus Independent Entrepreneurship: A Cross-National Analysis of Individual Entrepreneurial Behavior.* Tjalling C . Koopmans Institute Discussion Paper Series 11-04, Utrecht School of Economics, Utrecht University . retrieved 20151101 from https://www.uu.nl/sites/default/files/rebo_use_dp_2011_11-04.pdf

Bosma, N., Wennekers, S. & Amorós, J. E. (2012). *The Global Entrepreneurship Monitor 2011 Extended report: entrepreneurs and entrepreneurial employees across the globe.* http://www .gemconsortium.org/report

Bosma,N . Stam. E , Wennekers , S . (2012b) *Entrepreneurial Employee Activity: A Large Scale International Study,* Utrecht School of Economics, Tjalling C . Koopmans Research Institute, Discussion Paper Series 12-12, retrieved 20151208 from

https://www.researchgate.net/publication/254455562_Entrepreneurial_Employee_Activity_A_Large_Sc
ale_International_Study

Singer, S., Amoros, J.E., Moska, D. & GERA (2015). *GEM Global Entrepreneurship Monitor 2014*.
retrieved 20160803 from www.gemconsortium.org/report,

An intrapreneur's reality

Deci, E . & Ryan, R . (2000) Intrinsic and Extrinsic Motivations: Classic Definitions and DOI 10
.1006/ceps.1999.1020, *Contemporary Educational Psychology* 25, 54–67 (2000)
retrieved 20160305 from
https://mmrg.pbworks.com/f/Ryan,+Deci+00.pdf

Deci, E. & Ryan, R. (2010 July-Aug). intervju av Karen McCally, *Rochester Review 72*, (6), Rochester
University Self-Determined What motivates you? Two Rochester experimental psychologists are challenging
some cherished assumptions, retrieved 20160305 from
http://www.rochester.edu/pr/Review/V72N6/0401_feature1.html

Different types of innovation

The concept of innovation comes from Latin innovation, "Renew, bring something new", and according
to the Swedish National Encyclopedia (2016), it is "a process through which new ideas, behaviors and
approaches win entrances into a society and then spread there", retrieved 20160501

An established definition in the Oslo-manual, OECD 1997: ' An '*innovation*' is the implementation of
a new or significantly improved product (goods or service), or process, a new marketing method, or a
new organizational method in business practices, workplace organization or external relations

Schumpeter Joseph (1942) retrieved 20160401 from https://sv.wikipedia.org/wiki/Joseph_Schumpeter

Gratzer Karl (2004), interview by Jonas Gustafsson . Schumpeter Joseph, entreprenörskapsfältets första
och största kändis: "Entreprenörens roll är tidsbegränsad'. *Esbri* 2004-06-09 retrieved 20160401 from
http://www.esbri.se/artikel_visa.asp?id=233

The importance of the work climate for creativity and innovation

Ekvalls (1990) definition of the concept of organizational climate "Beteenden, attityder och känslostämningar som karakteriserar livet i organisationen'. *Idéer, organisationsklimat och ledningsfilosofi,* Stockholm: Nordstedts förlag .

Ekvall, G.(2007) intervju av Bøe Sigrid, Kreativiteten får inte plats på jobbet, *Dagens Nyheter* 2007-08-25, retrieved 20161005 from, http://www.dn.se/insidan/ kreativiteten-far-inte-plats-pa-jobbet/, de tio faktorerna, and:

Ekvall, G.(1997). Organizational conditions and levels of creativity. *Creativity and Innovation Management, 6* (4), 195-205. doi: 10.1111/1467-8691.00070, retrieved 20151030 from https://www.deepdyve.com/lp/wiley/organizational-conditions-and-levels-of-creativity-mxRPFhsEza?articleList=%2Fsearch%3Fauthor%3DG%25C3%25B6ran%2BEkvall

Ekvall, G . (2000) Management and Organizational Philosophies and practices as stimulants or blocks to creative behaviour: a study of engineers . *Creativity and Innovation Management, 9,* retrieved 20151030 from https://www.deepdyve.com/lp/wiley/management-and-organizational-philosophies-and-practices-as-stimulants-rNv1vmrNjj

Isaksen, S . G . & Ekvall, G . (2010) . Managing for innovation: the two faces of tension in creative climates, *Creativity and Innovation Management, 19*(2). doi:10.1111/j.1467-8691.2010.00558 , retrieved 20151201 from http://citeseerx.ist.psu.edu/viewdoc/download?doi=10.1.1.466.8786&rep=rep1&type=pdf

Motivation leads to creativity

Maslow, A . H . *(1943) . A Theory of Human Motivation,* initially in *Psychological Review, 50, 370-396,* retrieved 20160425 from http://psychcentral.com/classics/Maslow/motivation.htm

Maslow, A. H. (1954). *Motivation and personality,* Reprinted from the English Edition by Harper & Row, Publishers 1954, Abraham H . Maslow 1970 http://s-f-walker.org.uk/pubsebooks/pdfs/Motivation_and_Personality-Maslow.pdf

Deci, E. L., & Ryan, R. M. (1985). *Intrinsic motivation and self-determination in human behavior .* New York: Plenum.

Deci, E . & Ryan, R . (2000) . Intrinsic and Extrinsic Motivations: Classic Definitions and New directions

. *Contemporary Educational Psychology, 25,* 54–67. doi 10.1006/ceps.1999.1020, retrieved 20160301 from https://mmrg.pbworks.com/f/Ryan,+Deci+00.pdf

Deci, E.L & Ryan, R.M. (2000b). Self-determination Theory and the Facilitation of Intrinsic Motivation, Social Development, and Well-Being . *American Psychologist, 55,* 68–78, retrieved 20160301 from http://citeseerx.ist.psu.edu/viewdoc/download?doi=10.1.1.529.4370&rep=rep1&type=pdf

Pink, D. H. (2009). *Drive: the surprising truth about what motivates us,* New York: Riverhead Books.

Gagné, M . & Deci, (2005 April 14) . Self-determination theory and work motivation *Journal of organizational Behavior. 26,* 331-362 online Wiley InterScience, doi: 10.1002/job.322, retrieved 20160320 from http://onlinelibrary.wiley.com/doi/10.1002/job.322/abstract

Hennessey, B. A. & Amabile, T. M. (2009 Oct 19). Creativity, *Annual Review of Psychology, 61,* 569-598, (2010). doi10.1146/annurev.psych.093008.100416, retrieved 20160215 from http://papers.ssrn.com/sol3/papers.cfm?abstract_id=1601146

Intrapreneurs are driven by intrinsic motivation

Amabile, T. M. & Kramer, S. (2011). *The Progress Principle: Using Small Wins to Ignite Joy, Engagement, and Creativity at Work.* Harvard Business Review Press: Boston.

Amabile, T. M. & Kramer, S. (2012). How leaders kill meaning at work. *McKinsey Quarterly* (2012 Jan), retrieved 20160215 from http://www.mckinsey.com/global-themes/leadership/how-leaders-kill-meaning-at-work

The intrapreneurial team

Pinchot III, G. & Pellman, R. (1999). *Intrapreneuring in Action: A Handbook for Business Innovation.* Berrett-Koehler Publishers: San Francisco. ċtation "The best teams are cross-functional or cross-disciplinary. Most teams are led by one intrapreneur, but all the members of the team can be called intrapreneurs as long as each understands the whole dream and is continually working to find better ways to make it happen'

Management is the key to intrapreneurial success

Bosma, N., Stam, E., & Wennekers, S. (2010). Intrapreneurship - an international study . Scientific Analysis of Entrepreneurship and SMEs (2010 Jan 12) . EIM Research Report Intrapreneurship_v9 .doc: Zoetermeer, retrieved 20151101 from

http://citeseerx.ist.psu.edu/viewdoc/download?doi=10.1.1.333.6885&rep=rep1&type=pdf

Successful and credible leadership

Kouzes, J. and Posner, B. (1987). *The Leadership Challenge- How to make extraordinary things happens in organizations,* San Francisco: Jossey-Bass. (5th Ed. 2012)

Kouzes, J. and Posner, B. (2010) *The Truth about Leadership: The No-Fads, Heart-of-the-Matter Facts You Need to Know.* New York: John Wiley & Sons, Inc. (Ledarskapets sanningar 2011, Ashing translation . Malmö: Liber)

Kouzes , J . M . & Posner, B . Z . (2003) . excerpt *Five practices of exemplary leadership,* John Wiley & Sons, Inc, retrieved 20160815 from

http://www.meridianleadershipinstitute.com/media/5Practices_article.pdf

The importance of positive emotions for creativity and innovation

Fredrickson. B.L.. (2010). *Positivity- Groundbreaking research to release your inner optimist and thrive.* Oneworld: Oxford .

Fredrickson. B.L.. (2000). The undoing effect of positive emotions. *Motivation and Emotions* 2000 nr 24 . doi:10.1023/A:1010796329158, retrieved 20151001 from

https://www.ncbi.nlm.nih.gov/pmc/articles/PMC3128334/

Fredrickson. B.L. (2001). The Role of Positive Emotions in Positive Psychology The Broaden-and-Build Theory of positive emotions. *American Psychologist, 56* (3), (2001 March), doi 10.1037/0003-066x.56 .3.218, retrieved 20151001 from https://www.ncbi.nlm.nih.gov/pmc/articles/PMC3122271/

Fredrickson . B .L . (2013) . Updated Thinking on Positivity Ratios Online *American Psychologist First Publication,* July 15, 2013. doi: 10.1037/a0033584, retrieved 20160101 from

http://www.unc.edu/peplab/publications/Fredrickson%202013%20Updated%20Thinking.pdf

Fredrickson. B.L & Losada M.F. (2005). (Om Positivitetskvoten) Positive affect and the complex dynamics of human flourishing . *American Psychologist 60* (7) (2005 Oct), doi:10 .1037/0003-066X.60.7.678 /, retrieved 20151001 from https://www.ncbi.nlm.nih.gov/pmc/articles/PMC3126111/

Losada, M.F. & Heapy, E. (2004). The Role of Positivity and Connectivity in the Performance of Business Teams A Nonlinear Dynamics Model, Meta Learning . *American Behavioral Scientist* 2004; 47; 740, doi: 10.1177/0002764203260208, retrieved 20151001 from http://abs.sagepub.com/content/47/6/740

Sokal, A .D ., Brown, N . & Friedman, H .L . (2013) . (Nick Brown was a student in applied positive psychology who took the initiative to question the positivity ratio) "Positive psychology and romantic scientism" . *American Psychologist,* 69 (6), 636–637 .doi:10.1037/a0037390, retrieved 20160101 from https://en.wikipedia.org/wiki/Critical_positivity_ratio

Kouzes, J . and Posner, B . (2010) . *The Truth about Leadership: The No-Fads, Heart-of-the-Matter Facts You Need to Know* . New York: John Wiley & Sons, Inc . (Ledarskapets sanningar 2011, Ashing translation, Malmö: Liber)

Amabile, T.M. & Kramer, S. (2011). *The Progress Principle: Using Small Wins to Ignite Joy, Engagement, and Creativity at Work.* Harvard Business Review Press: Boston .

The importance of the brain for the ability to innovate

Barrett, L.F. (2009) intervju av Per Snaprud Att resonera med skräcken *Forskning & Framsteg,* 2009-08-05 online (refers to a study: Affect is a form of cognition: A neurobiological analysis, Duncan, S.& Barrett, LF. *Cogn Emot ,* (6),1184-1211, 2007 Sep 21), retrieved 20160901 from http://fof.se/tidning/2009/6/att-resonera-med-skracken

Different parts of the brain and how they affect us

1 . Information about the brain is mainly retrieved from the Sahlgrenska Academy (Gothenburg University) encyclopedia " Nervsystemet .se".,), retrieved 20160101 from http://nervsystemet.se/nsd/index.php?node=1
Prefrontal cortex *PFC:* http://nervsystemet.se/nsd/structure_382
The nervous system, http://nervsystemet.se/nsd/structure_631
https://sv.wikipedia org/wiki/Prefrontala_cortex

Basal ganglia: http://nervsystemet.se/nsd/structure_68

The limbic system: http://nervsystemet.se/nsd/structure_813

The Reptilian/brainstem: http://nervsystemet.se/nsd/structure_136

https://sv.wikipedia.org/wiki/Hj%C3%A4rnstammen

Sapolsky, R . M . (2004) . The Frontal Cortex and the Criminal Justice System . *Philosophical Transactions of the Royal Society of London . Series B, Biological Sciences, 359* (1451), 1787–96, (2004 Nov 29): doi: 10.1098/rstb.2004.1547,

retrieved 20160116 from http://rstb.royalsocietypublishing.org/content/359/1451/1787

Kumar, A., Bahuguna, J., Aertsen, A. (2015 a). article 'Are we wired to be natural naysayers'? *KTH,* New & *Events/News,* KTH, 20150527, online retrieved 201510901 from

https://www.kth.se/en/aktuellt/nyheter/are-we-wired-to-be-natural-naysayers-1.569228

Kumar, A ., Bahuguna, J ., Aertsen, A . (2015 b) . article To Go or Not to Go? *Bernstein center, University of Freiburg News,* 20150427online, retrieved 20151004 from

https://www.bcf.uni-freiburg.de/news/publications/20150427-to-go-or-not-to-go

Graybiel, A . M . (2013) . interview by Nicholette Zeliadt, QnAs with Ann M . Graybiel . *Proc Natl Acad Sci U S A.;* 110(43), (2013 Sept 9) . online, doi:10.1073/pnas.1315012110, retrieved 20161001 from https://www.ncbi.nlm.nih.gov/pmc/articles/PMC3808670/

Gospic K . & Ingvar M . (2011 a) . article *Karolinska Institutet news.cision. com,*"Känsla för rättvisa inbyggd i hjärnan", 20110504 (refers to a study *Limbic justice—amygdala involvement in immediate rejection in the Ultimatum Game* by Gospic K, Mohlin E, Fransson P,Petrovic P,Johannesson M, Ingvar M.) , retrieved 20160118 from http://ki.se/nyheter/kansla-for-rattvisa-inbyggd-i-hjarnan

Gospic, K . (2011 b) . intervju av interview by Tomas Dalström, *International meetings*(2011-12) , retrieved 20160118 from http://www.meetingsinternational.se/articles.php?id=248#.V_u3YP-mLRdh

Willpower

Mischel, Walter (1972). "Marshmallovstudien' (The Marshmallow study), Cognitive and attentional mechanisms in delay of gratification av Mischel, W., Ebbesen, E. B.& Raskoff Zeiss, A. *Journal of Personality and Social Psychology, 21* (2), 204-218, (1972 Feb), retrieved 20151208 from http://dx.doi.org/10.1037/h0032198

Baumeister, R (1998). https://sv.wikipedia.org/wiki/Egodepletion. refers to

Baumeister, R. F., Bratslavsky, E., Muraven, M., & Tice, D. M. "Ego depletion: Is the active self a limited resource?". *Journal of Personality and Social Psychology, 74* (5), 1252–1265. doi: 10.1037//0022-3514.74.5.1252, retrieved 20160805 from https://faculty.washington.edu/jdb/345/345%20Articles/Baumeister%20et%20al.%20(1998).pdf

Gailliot, M. & Baumeister R.F. (2007). The Physiology of Willpower: Linking Blood Glucose to Self-Control. doi: 10.1177/1088868307303030 *Pers Soc Psychol Rev, 11* (4), 303-327 (2007 Nov), abstract retrieved 20160812 from http://psr.sagepub.com/content/11/4/303

Baumeister, R., & Tierney, J. (2011). *Willpower: Rediscovering the Greatest Human Strength* . New York: Penguin Press .

Glaser, J. & Knowles,E.D. (2008). Implicit Motivation to Control Prejudice *Journal of Experimental Social Psychology, 44*, 164-172, (2007 Jan 18) retrieved 20160915 from https://gspp.berkeley .edu/assets/uploads/research/pdf/GlaserKnowles08.pdf,

Muraven, M. (2012). *Ego-depletion: Theory and evidence.* Oxford Handbook of Motivation . Oxford: Oxford University Press (2012 Sept) .
doi 10.1093/oxfordhb/9780195399820.013.0007 retrieved 20160801

Inzlicht, M, Schmeichel, B.J (2012). *What Is Ego Depletion? Toward a Mechanistic Revision of the Resource Model* of Self-Control. *Perspectives on Psychological Science, 7* (5), 450-463, (2012 Sept). doi:10 .1177/1745691612454134, retrieved 20160914

Inzlicht, M, Schmeichel, B.J & Macrae, C.N. (2013). Why self-control seems (but may not be) limited *Trends in Cognitive Sciences, 18* (3), (2014 March), retrieved 20160914 from http://dx.doi.org/10 .1016/j.tics.2013.12.009,

Francis, Z.L. & Inzlicht, M. (2016). *Proximate and ultimate causes of ego depletion.* Hirt E. (Ed.), *Self-Regulation and Ego Control,* 373-398. New York: Elsevier, retrieved 20160914 from https://static1 .squarespace.com/static/550b09ea-4b0147d03eda40d/t/57c8d9716a49630f05b1e020/1472780764171/ Francis+%26+Inzlicht%2C+2016.pdf

Patience and resilience

Gladwell Malcolm (2008). *Outliers: The Story of Success*, Little, Brown and Company, Boston, Massachusetts, USA

Krishnan, S .S . & Sitaraman, R .K (2012) . Video Stream Quality Impacts Viewer Behavior: Inferring Causality Using Quasi-Experimental Designs *IEEE/ ACM Transactions on Networking, 21* (6), (2013 Dec*). https://psyciencia.com/ wp-content/uploads/2012/11/Video-Stream-Quiality-Impacts-Viewer-Behaior.pdf retrieved 20160101*

The importance of the brain for the development of habits

Calakos, N . & O'Hare, J.K. (2016). Why are habits so hard to break? Getting hooked changes the brain, scientists find, *Medical Express*, (2016 Jan 21) ref: *Neuron* gm: Duke University (based on "Pathway-Specific Striatal Substrates for Habitual Behavior", O'Hare, J.K., Ade, K.K., Sukharnikova, T., Van Hooser, S.D ., Yin, H.H ., Calakos, N ., *Neuron*, (2016 Jan 21). doi: 10.1016/j .neuron.2015.12.032, retrieved 20161101 from http://medicalxpress.com/news/2016-01-habits-hard-brain-scientists.html,

Graybiel, A . M . (2013) . intervju av Nicholette Zeliadt QnAs with Ann M . Graybiel . *Proc Natl Acad Sci U S A, 110* (43), (2013 Sept 9) . online doi: 10.1073/pnas.1315012110 retrieved 20161001 from https://www.ncbi.nlm.nih.gov/pmc/articles/PMC3808670/,

Olson, L . (2011) Hjärnans hårda skola, intervju av Ola Danielsson *Medicinsk vetenskap 3* gm *Karolinska Institutet Forskning* online 20150818 retrieved 20160805 from http://ki.se/forskning/hjarnans-harda-skola,

Habitual thinking and thinking traps

"The Dual ProcessTheory" https://en.wikipedia.org/wiki/Dual_process_theory
Stanovich, K.& West, R.F . (2000). Individual differences in reasoning: Implications for the rationality debate? *Behavorial and Brain Sciences, 23* (5), 645–726, retrieved 20160801 from http://psy2.ucsd .edu/~mckenzie/StanovichBBS.pdf

Kahneman, D . & Tversky, A . (1979) . Prospect Theory: An Analysis of Decision under Risk *Econometrica, 47(2)*, 263-291,(1979 March) , retrieved 20160801 from https://www.princeton.edu/ ~kahneman/docs/Publications/prospect_theory.pdf

Kahneman, D . (2011) *Thinking, fast and slow* Penguin Random House: UK (2012)
Conscious and unconscious attitudes

1 . I have downloaded information about various psychological schools:
Cognitive Psychology: https://sv.wikipedia.org/wiki/Kognitiv_psykologi
Psychodynamic Psychology: https://sv.wikipedia.org/wiki/Psykodynamisk_psykoterapi
Behaviorist psychology: https://sv.wikipedia.org/wiki/Behaviorism
Neurological psychology: https://sv.wikipedia.org/wiki/Neuropsykologi

Crick, F . & Koch, C . (1990) . Towards a neurobiological theory of consciousness, *The Neurosciences, 2*, 263- 275, retrieved 20160501 from http://authors.library.caltech.edu/40352/1/148.pdf

Crick, F. (1994). *The Astonishing Hypothesis: The Scientific Search For The Soul*. Scribner: New York, retrieved 20160501 from https://en.wikipedia.org/wiki/The Astonishing Hypothesis

Koch, C . (2014a) . Is Consciousness Universal? Scientific American (2014 Jan 1) retrieved, 20160502 from https://www.scientificamerican.com/article/is-consciousness-universal/

Koch, C . (2014b). A Neuroscientist's Radical Theory of How Networks Become Conscious, intervju av Brandon Kiem, *Wired.com* (2014 Nov 13)
retrieved 20160502 from https://www.wired.com/2013/11/christof-koch-panpsychism-consciousness/

Trust and understanding are crucial

Janssen, C.(1981) . *Personlig dialektik – självcensur, outsiderupplevelser och integration*. Liber Förlag: Stockholm (2nd Ed. 1975), as well as clarifications in interview with Bengt Lindström, CEO of Fyrarummaren AB, 20161031, www.fyrarummaren.se

Ahuja, G . & Lampert, C . M . Entrepreneurship in the Large Corporation: A Longitudinal Study of How Established Firms Create Breakthrough Inventions. *Strategic Management Journal, 22*(6-7), 521–543, (2001 Jun-Jul). doi: 10.1002/smj.176, retrieved 20160301 from https://datapro.fiu.edu/campusedge/files/documenturl/morrislampc031314083928.pdf

Kalling, T . (2007) The Lure of Simplicity: Learning Perspectives on Innovation *European Journal of Innovation Management, 10*(1), 65-89. doi.org/10.1108/14601060710720555, retrieved 20160301 from http://www.emeraldinsight.com/doi/abs/10.1108/14601060710720555

Denti, L.& Kreuger, M. Innovationsarbetets hinder *Tidningen Chef* online 20151109/, retrieved 20160101 from http://chef.se/innovationsarbetets-hinder

Engberg, I . & Lundström, S.(2014) *Att skapa en intraprenör – en studie om den organisatoriska kontextens betydelse för intraprenöriellt beteende* , a Master's thesis, Södertörns högskola, Department of Social Sciences, retrieved 20151101 from www.diva-portal.se/smash/get/diva2:729972/FULLTEXT01.pdf

Sinha, N. & Srivastava, K.B.L. (2013). Association of Personality, Work Values and Socio-cultural Factors with Intrapreneurial Orientation, *Journal of Entrepreneurship*, *22*(1), 97–113, (2013 March 1) doi:10.1177/0971355712469186, retrieved 20160101 from https://www.researchgate.net/profile/Kailash_Srivastava2/publication/258154228_Association_of_ Personality_Work_Values_and_Socio- cultural_Factors_with_Intrapreneurial_Orientation/links/5811a7fb08ae009606be8403.pdf

Ett nytt managementkoncept för kontinuerlig innovation

Schwab, K . (2016) . The Fourth Industrial Revolution: what it means, how to respond . *World Economic Forum* online (14 January 2016) , retrieved 20161101 from https://www.weforum.org/agenda/2016/01/the-fourth-industrial-revolution-what-it-means-and-how- to-respond/